The Perspective of Women Project Management Professionals

IPEK SAHRA OZGULER

Publisher: Ipek Sahra Ozguler
Editor: Bahar Atlamaz Barutcu
Cover Design: Sevgi Onbay

i

Dedication

To every project manager who helps forge a gender equal world.

Contents

iv

Acknowledgments

Creating and publishing a book based on experiences and observations made in the real business world through conducting interviews with distinguished women project management professionals is an amazing journey.

I would like to thank to everyone who took a part of in this journey alongside me, believed in my dream and vision, showed tremendous support and inspired me.

Special thanks to each interviewee, listed below, who understood my book project and my passion, was a unique part of it, took time from their busy schedules to answer my questions, shared their project management history for this book. Without them this dream could not have been realized.

- Annie Sheehan / Australia
- Alenka Gruden / Slovenia
- Angelica Maria Larios Arias / Mexico
- Antje Lehmann Benz / Germany
- Carla Fair Wright / USA
- Cecilia Boggi / Argentina
- Claude El Nakhel Khalil (Dr.) / Lebanon
- Deena Gordon Parla / USA
- Deanna Landers / USA
- Diana Milena Ramirez Leon / Colombia
- Diane Dromgold / Australia
- Emma Ruth Arnaz Pemberton / United Kingdom

- Jane Farley / New Zealand
- Jennifer Young Baker / USA
- Lavetta T Stevenson / USA
- Lori Nevin / USA
- LuAnn Piccard / USA
- Malgorzata Kusyk / Poland
- Margarida Goncalves (Dr.) / Portugal
- Merete Munch Lange / Norway
- Mona Fazel / Iran
- Raji Sivaraman / Singapore
- Ramesh Vahidi / United Kingdom
- Ruth Pearce / USA
- Sandy Lawrence / USA
- Teresa Knudson / USA
- Vanita Bhoola (Dr.) / India
- Viviane De Paula / Brazil
- Yvonne Butler / Australia

I greatly appreciate the advice and support of David Pells, managing editor of Project Management World Journal, a global eJournal for program and project management, Sevgi Onbay, who shared her exclusive artistic talent during the designing phase, and Bahar Barutcu.

Finally, even bigger thanks to my mother and my primary school teacher Sukran Guner for believing in me more than anyone.

Foreword

When I first heard the proposal for this book of interviews, my response was somewhat reserved. I was confident that it would result in some outstanding interviews, many highlighting the challenges and successes of women in the project management field. Knowing some of the interviewees, I expected the interviews to reflect professional knowledge and experiences. Nevertheless, I was concerned that the results might limit the audience to women. I was wrong! The concept for this book was brilliant!

Yes, the questions are asked and answers provided that highlight the challenges and roadblocks that many women still face in too many organizations and on too many projects. Gender bias is real. Women are still overlooked, underpaid, challenged to over perform, with their efforts too often discounted. These are important topics that should be highlighted. The women who are interviewed have achieved success in spite of the many roadblocks; their stories are both enlightening and empowering. Their stories should be celebrated. This book is spectacular for that reason alone.

But it is also much more. The interviewees describe their personal journeys, the reasons why and how they got involved with project management in the first place. And why they went on to pursue graduate degrees, professional certifications and even leadership roles in the PM profession. They discuss issues they face as project managers and project team members, issues ranging from lack of adequate support by senior executives, incompetent or unknowledgeable sponsors, lack of adequate resources, lack of authority, organizational immaturity, bureaucratic attitudes and many other factors. They discuss current pressures and risks facing many projects, including rapidly changing environmental factors including the now well-known volatility, uncertainty, complexity and ambiguity (VUCA) conditions that we are all so familiar with.

These are issues facing all project managers and professionals, male or female. The interviews in this book nearly all reflect a deep understanding and knowledge about the full range of issues facing most people in the PM profession. Their answers are informative and should be useful to many readers. Most importantly, these interviews tell personal stories that many of us can relate to, from the drivers early in our careers to the challenges faced along the stressful path in the difficult field that is project management. These are important stories.

I also thought it might be more appropriate to have a woman write this foreword for a book of interviews about women in project management, a book I thought was about and for women. I was wrong about that as well. These interviews are for both women and men to read, perhaps men most of all. Men must recognize that the future requires change. It's time for gender bias and inequality to be fully and completely discarded. It's time to move on.

Men have been controlling governments, economies, industries, organizations and projects for centuries. Now we have massive global economic, environmental and social problems. Projects continue to fail at high rates in nearly all industries. New approaches are absolutely needed. As the old saying goes, if we continue to do things the same way and expect different results, we are delusional. It is time that we embrace the talents, energies, knowledge and expertise among 100% of the world's population.

The women featured in this book are experts and leaders, professionals, executives and team members. They know what they are talking about. We should all listen to them. Their stories are for all of us.

I have known and worked with Ipek for many years. I respect her passion for the PM profession and applaud what she has accomplished here. I am honored to provide these few comments and have been humbled by the experience. Especially while writing them on International Women's Day.

David L. Pells
PMI Fellow, HonFAPM, FISIPM
Editor, PM World Journal

8 March 2020
Addison, Texas, USA

Introduction and Summary

From November 2019 to February 2020 I have conducted twenty-nine interviews for my book project "The Perspective of Women Project Management Professionals" (published on Amazon Kindle, March 2020). The interviewees were purposely selected based on the nationalities to gain views and valuable insights from different perspectives globally. The aim of realizing this book project is to share the interviewees' opinions without including my own comments. It is surprising to find out that the majority of the answers were similar across different regions of the world. I think that the perspectives of women project management professionals are more or less similar. This comment can be evaluated further in another project.

The countries included are Argentina, Australia, Brazil, Colombia, Germany, India, Iran, Lebanon, Mexico, New Zealand, Norway, Poland, Portugal, Singapore, Slovenia, United Kingdom, United States. The locations are in brief as follows;

LOCATION	PERCENTAGE
ASIA	14%
AUSTRALIA	14%
EUROPE	24%
NORTH AMERICA	38%
SOUTH AMERICA	10%

As part of the book, speaking with twenty-nine women project management professionals, I asked them nine questions about their project management career and experience. Each interviewee gave her own unique perspective based on her background, experience and culture. I wish that the readers who are willing to derive benefits from real career stories will enjoy the book.

First of all, the details of each interviewee' s career journey were asked. Their ways of starting to a project management career are varied: Chance or Deliberate. Almost all have the interviewees started their project management career by chance/accident than predetermination and concurrently they were not credentialed. Soon after beginning their career, the interviewees noticed the importance of doing a master degree in project management, gaining certification and volunteering, in order to catch advantage of opportunities and access to leadership position. Only two of the interviewees became deliberately a project manager.

The aim of the second question is to point out those reasons why the interviewees have chosen to become project management professional. The reasons are: passion for people management and project management, variety and diversity within project management field, the unique character of each project, enjoying problem solving, overcoming challenges while reaching a unique goal, opportunity to work in a dynamic environment through bringing different personalities and capabilities as a team, possibility of continuous learning, to improve the technical, interpersonal and interpersonal skills.

Robert Tew said that "the struggle you are in today is developing the strength you need tomorrow". Therefore, the next question tries to figure out obstacles women face in advancing their careers. The most important obstacles are gender inequality and gender bias. Some examples shared by the interviewees show that a woman may be underestimated and therefore should work harder because of her gender and prove repeatedly herself despite having several degrees, certifications and proven experience. A woman could be passed over for a less experienced or qualified man or a man could be assigned to the important or high visibility projects instead of a woman. Furthermore, a man could receive plenty of support compared to a woman.

Some general obstacles mentioned other than the gender issue are: stereotyping, racial bias, the difficulty of finding and/or applying appropriate tools and techniques, lack of clear communications, staff attitudes and bureaucracy with a resistance to change, to assess project success based on time and budget rather than assessing the value realized by the business for the resources invested, not to evaluate success factors tied to soft skills, not to offer any project management training, not to have a technical degree and/or background, high levels of uncertainty, not to possess authority in order to resolve conflicts, the lack of understanding of what project management actually is, to consider project management "operational" rather than "strategic" by other parties.

A few interviewees evaluated obstacles as challenges and opportunities. According them, new perspectives and values are offered through overpassing them. Only four interviewees, from South America, North America and Europe, said that there is no obstacle. Some of the interviewees stated that owning PMP credential allowed them to take advantage of interesting opportunities and access leadership positions.

Furthermore, the unwritten and unstated goals, policies, alliances, conflicts and values in the workplace should be considered. An understanding should be developed because of not all stakeholders are working to the greater good of the organization, as people have their own interests.

"Why it is important that more people in the project management area?" is another question to be considered. Project Management Institute stated that, today we are in the Project Economy in which people have the skills and capabilities they need to turn ideas into reality. Despite project management is one of the professions of the future and project managers are needed everywhere in order to bridge the gap from strategy to implementation, there is a worldwide shortage of project management professionals. PMI estimated "the talent gap could result in a potential loss of some $207.9 billion in GDP through 2027". Project Management Job Growth and Talent Gap 2017–2027 reveals that through 2027, the project management labor force is expected to grow by 33 percent. That means 22 million new jobs will be created during the next 10 years and by 2027 organisations will need nearly 88 million individuals working in project management-oriented roles, even with Gartner's prediction last year that 80% of all project management support or PMO tasks by 2030, will be replaced by the growing use of AI, machine learning and robotic process automation. Moreover, the Anderson Economic Group (AEG) analysis finds the project management profession will outperform total U.S. job growth over the next decade, creating millions of new positions that pay highly-competitive wages.

The interviewees argued that project managers should have good project management skills, be trained more and more professionally, be an agent of transformation and permanent development in any organization and in the world, bring holistic perspectives, a deep curiosity and broad skill sets for the following reasons:

- The world, environment, and market have been volatile, uncertain, complex and competitive.

- There is a pressure in order to be more agile, innovative and adaptable to change. One of the interviewees argued that "the field of project management has begun to change from a strictly traditional only approach to a hybrid agile approach".

- The project management profession has a pretty poor reputation, because of some unskilled project managers.

Many interviewees said that project management is a lifetime skill needed in whatever we do for example wedding, parenting etc.

Only one argued that it is not as important that more people work in project management area.

It is essential to encourage more people to pursue project management as a career. How we can achieve this is explained by the twenty-nine women. First of all, the target group such as young people, pupils, university students should be determined and reached out to build awareness of this profession. There are some initiatives in order to achieve this. For example, the aim of the initiative "Projects in Bloom" is to spread project culture among pupils. PMI Education Foundation is an organization which brings project management skills to the youth, particularly the five to nineteen age group. Another initiative called gameScrum is a way to teach delivering projects through playing.

To contribute to the economy, humanity, technology and the world through project management is tremendously rewarding and endless. In order to pursue more people, it should be shown:

- The attractiveness of project management,

- The inevitable challenges and difficulties in project management,

- Positive impacts in the lives of people in general and in organizations,

- Being a registered professional brings more prestige.

The top issues facing project managers today are evaluated based on the interviewees' answers. Most of the top issues are the reasons of why it is important to work more people in the project management area. The top issues are listed below:

- The world is moving very fast. The organizations are facing the challenges of fast paced technology (Artificial Intelligence etc.) and trying to keep up with the emergency trends. Only one found these challenges exciting.

- The nature of projects is complex, challenging, uncertain, unpredictable and full of constant-change. The project managers should handle these projects and obtain positive results through balancing all elements, choosing the right project management way, using the appropriate interpersonal skills in order to deal different characteristics and cultures.

- The project success is measured by time, scope, budget and quality instead of value and benefits realization.

- Roles and responsibilities are not clear. There is lack of understanding and respecting project management and their value.

- There are some unskilled project managers.

One of the interviewees (Poland), argued that "companies need project practitioners with leadership and business intelligence skills" and supported her argument such that, according to PMI's Pulse of the Profession® report, when organizations focus on all three skill sets (technical, leadership, strategic and business management expertise) 40 percent more of their projects meet goals and original business intent. As much as 39% of respondents of a survey conducted in New Zealand, also similar to European conditions, highlighted that leading change in their organisation is a top gap, while 34% identified difficult conversations and conflict management as missing key competences. Another 30% of research participants mentioned the importance of political 'smarts' and resolving 'gray' issues. And 27% responded that communication is still a challenge.

Another top issue mentioned by Carla Fair Wright is Power Stress. She said that "It is a silent health issue that results from the constant exercise of influence and sense of responsibility in leadership position. This is a key symptom of the "Sacrifice Syndrome". According to Richard Boyatzis and Annie McKee, writers of "Resonant Leadership", Sacrifice Syndrome can occur over time because of a number of factors, including pressure to get results, heavy responsibilities, the perpetual need to influence people and feelings of loneliness".

To define stereotypes attached to project managers is another questioned subject. Based on the answers of the interviewees, the project management stereotype is classified as positive, negative and neutral. Two of the interviewees are mentioned positive stereotypes. The positive stereotypes are the following: analytical and a good manager, servant leaders.

The negative stereotypes attached to the project managers are summarized below.

- Just an administrative role. The roles are only operational, not strategic. The other terminologies used instead of the terminology "administrator" are as following: librarians, a kind of secretary.

- Unwanted disrupters who don't get anything done.

- Nagging people that just get in their way of doing work.

- They don't want any change in the project.

The characteristics of a project manager are: structured (methodic, rigid, bureaucratic, command and control), meeting-happy (meeting note taker, meeting organizer), task focused, detailed, inflexible (for example they always think/talk about processes and tools), not technical and at last, male dominated.

Cecilia Boggi from Argentina shared this gender issue in number. According to studies conducted by the Project

Management Institute (PMI), it is estimated that only about 30% of the world's project managers are women. She continued that "the areas or industries that have the greatest impact on project management tend to be predominantly masculine". (such as IT and construction)

Lavetta Stevenson from USA and Ramesh Vahidi from United Kingdom are not aware of a common stereotype attached to project managers. Yvonne Butler from Australia and Margarida Golcalves from Portugal stated that there is no stereotype.

Lastly, the importance of International Women's Day (IWD) is explained by the interviewees. A very obvious observation from the interviews is that equality is still an important issue. It is a global day to remember women who fought and gave their lives, support all women around the world that are still fighting, to deeply understand and celebrate women's achievements, provide the inspiration as role models to the next generation, raise awareness. Most of the interviewees emphasized that togetherness brings power and difference.

According to UN.org, the 2019 theme is, "Think equal, build smart, innovate for change", focusing on innovative ways women can advance gender equality and empowerment in terms of "social protection systems, access to public services and sustainable infrastructure".

In the project management profession, about 30% of project managers are female, and only 1% of females are likely to become a project director or board members compared with 4% of males, and reportedly there is 23.1% pay gap between males and females.

As Emma Ruth Arnaz Pemberton from United Kingdom stated that "we now need to start moving forward from this point of view, acknowledge the progress, and focus on the future".

At the end of the interviews, each interviewee shares their own message. If you want to know more about the interviews, read the remaining part of this book.

Thanks to each interviewee for sharing her life story and opinions for this project.

Annie Sheehan

Australia

Silicon Valley Alliances / Global Consultant

Q1•Describe your journey as a project management professional.

My first career was as an Information Technology specialist. I started with an international software house as an analyst/ programmer. I enjoyed the client-facing aspects more than the technology and enjoyed consulting, systems configuration and problem-solving more than coding. I ended up as a senior consultant working internationally and using project management skills to implement financial services systems for clients. I received my first project management training and enjoyed applying it a lot. In 1999, I decided to specialize in project management and do that as a full-time career rather than as a dimension of my role.

I also project managed my own wedding back in the 1990s. I had Gantt charts and the budget on a spreadsheet. I worked out the plan, the budget, the schedule, identified the stakeholders, assessed the risk and did all the organizing. Difficult stakeholders were managed (many of them were family members) and given specific jobs to do. The wedding event went really well and I had such a sense of achievement at the end of it because everyone enjoyed it. We achieved our essential scope items, were within budget and the quality was exactly

1

what we wanted. This experience stayed with me and I wondered how I could replicate this in real life.

I've ended up in a variety of firms performing numerous project management, consulting and coaching roles. In the corporate world, my most senior positions were as a General Manager and a Program Director, which were more strategic and transformational.

I decided to become an independent consultant about a year ago so that I could embrace the work I enjoy the most. This includes advising executives on their projects, coaching, facilitation and training.

Q2· Why did you choose to become a project management professional?

I have a passion for people and project management. I love the variety within the field of project management and the fact that there are always new ways of delivering, so I am continually learning.

Q3· Have you encountered any related obstacles in advancing your career?

The biggest challenges I have faced in my career have been:

- *Being passed over for a less experienced or qualified male. The male in all cases had better sponsorship and than I did. So my advice for women in project management who would like to advance in their careers is to get coaching, sponsorship and advocacy for roles, preferably from an influential male mentor.*

- *Being part-time and a parent. Even when flexible work is offered, it has been dependent on my individual line manager and their values and views on flexible working. My advice is to manage expectations upfront, be reliable, deliver value and be*

2

flexible with your time. Have a work-life blend approach. If you need to support a family member during standard working hours, be prepared to catch up on your work during non-standard hours. It's a balance of give and take.

I have experienced inconsistent support trying to work part-time or flexibly when you have a family. I have seen plenty of support offered to men who need to parent; they are often seen as valiant heroes. I have not seen the same support standard provided to women; perhaps societal values mean that women are expected to parent and work and not ask for help.

Q4• Why is it important that more people work in the project management area?

There is a global shortage of people with good project management skills. Approximately 25% of the world's economy is spent on projects and many of them still fail to deliver to the desired success criteria. I believe that everyone benefits from fundamental project management skills as it helps with so many work and life aspects. For example, many of my colleagues have done home renovations and have benefited from using project management skills to plan and execute their projects.

Q5• How can we encourage more people to pursue project management as a career?

I think the profession would benefit from being a registered profession, like accountants and lawyers. That way, it would carry more prestige and only qualified and experienced people could call themselves project managers.

Highlighting the benefits of project management as a career would be great. Hearing stories from project managers, what they've enjoyed and what they've achieved is inspiring and motivating.

Q6• What do you think are the top issues that project managers face today?

- *Unskilled people passing themselves off as project managers, giving experienced and credentialed project managers a bad name.*
- *The lack of understanding and respect for project management skills. Inexperienced stakeholders expect project managers to be super beings. If a PM is unable to articulate their value and demonstrate their work and how it is helping an organisation, they can be easily devalued and dismissed.*

Q7• Do you think there is a stereotype attached to project managers?

Many stakeholders see project managers as administrators who produce reports, rather than the problem-solving leaders that they really are.

Q8• Why is it important to celebrate international women's day?

To give women a voice to share their achievements and contribution to the world.

To recognize that women make up half the population of our planet and over 40% of the workforce, mainly in vital support roles.

Q9• On international women' s day, what is the most important message you offer to project management professionals?

Embrace diversity in all its forms. It brings richness to a team. Female project managers tend to bring a nurturing quality to the team. When the team feels protected and supported, they go the extra mile in driving for results.

Annie Sheehan

Annie is an internationally recognized expert in Project Management with over 25 years' experience in consulting and project delivery. A past president of PMI Melbourne Chapter, Annie is currently serving in a PMI Global role as a Region Mentor and is a Graduate of the Australian Institute of Company Directors. She is also a global consultant for the Silicon Valley Alliances, representing them in Australia.

During the last 10 years, Annie has focused on coaching executives in the process of becoming accountable as project sponsors to deliver business projects and achieve sustainable change. Using an agile mindset with established project delivery practices, Annie has help organisations find ways to deliver value in manageable chunks using simple, repeatable processes. Annie adopts creative approaches to solving her clients' problems, drawing from her extensive experience and tool kits.

Annie is certified as an Agile Certified Scrum Master and a Six Sigma Green Belt. She has achieved superior results in sponsor coaching, capability development and improving project delivery methodology for numerous blue-chip companies including National Australia Bank and AXA. She now works with clients across a range of industries and countries.

Annie is the author of the book "The Courageous Sponsor - How to overcome challenges to get your project done", due for release in early 2020. She is the co-author of "Turning Ideas into Impact – Insights from Silicon Valley consultants" published in February 2020.

Alenka Gruden
Slovenia

Proteam / Director

Q1• Describe your journey as a project management professional.

I still remember my first job because I was so excited to join one of the most growing and innovative company. I joined the biggest mobile operator in Slovenia. Can you imagine me, just finishing university, very curious and with the best possibility to learn more? It was amazing. Their vision was to be the first and the best in the field, not only in Slovenia but also in the region. Exciting! My first assignment was to take care for logistics. Very soon I realized that we need to redefine and simplify the processes and agreements. So, my superior decided this could be something that I could work on. And this is how I joined the world of Project Management. Of course, in the beginning, I was leading a project based on my intuition. Which was obviously good, since my first, not official project was successfully finished, and my superior decided that I should officially lead projects. I loved my new challenges and the fact that I need to learn something new every day. I was lucky to have a boss with knowledge and experiences in project management, and awareness on how important it is to have the right knowledge for the work that you are responsible for. Every year I had a chance to attend a course on Project Management, which

7

helped me a lot to learn new tools and techniques and lead projects better. I fell in love with leading projects from the beginning, and I am still in love with it. Therefore, I am still working in this profession. For every project, I feel like it is my child and I try to treat it so. For me, the most important aspect is to respect people and to build trust in teams. Projects need to be led transparently. A team needs to be collaborative and you, as the project manager, need to embrace and empower them. Your role is to listen to the team members and to remove all obstacles on the projects so that they can focus on the work to be done. For me, it is also important to learn as much as possible about the content the project is dealing with. I need to understand what the desired outcome is, what is the value and benefit for the company or the customer. In my more than 20 years of journey in project management field, I have been serving in different industries and there is one thing that I do the same, and that is; people first. I like challenges in my life, and I love working with people and these are the main reasons that I am still part of this complex, challenging, uncertain, unpredictable and full of constant-change profession.

Q2• Why did you choose to become a project management professional?

After ten years of experience in project management profession, I decided for the next step, to get official accreditation. This was my personal decision and the company I was working for decided, to support my decision. I heard from some professional project managers that PMI's PMP certificate is very difficult. This was an additional challenge for me, and I was even more eager to pass this exam and to become a PMP. I am still very proud to own this global credential. This was also a very important step for me because I realized that PMI has also a chapter in Slovenia. This was an amazing opportunity to network with professionals in my field and share experiences, knowledge and at the same time build a community of professional project managers. I became an active volunteer in PMI where I could serve in my profession. Volunteering is giving me the opportunity to learn new skills which I can then bring into my work life, or just gives me the opportunity to give back to the community. To serve people.

Q3• Have you encountered any related obstacles in advancing your career?

As a woman in project management, in the field of technology and IT environment where men dominate, was always challenging. I had to work and study harder than any man that I know in my profession. I had to repeatedly prove that I am an experienced and trustworthy project manager with great results. I admit it was hard but worth it. I had worked with many amazing and innovative teams and together we managed to bring great benefits and values to the company.

For the last few years since I've been working as an entrepreneur and at the same time, I am also a proud PMI volunteer. Many times it happens that these two roles become very confusing and hard to differentiate. I guess I need some improvements in this area.

Q4• Why is it important that more people work in the project management area?

The world is changing a lot and almost everything that we are doing today is some kind of a project. Anything that brings value to the company is a project. I believe that many occupations that we know today will be replaced by AI technology, but I believe that this will not happen to the project management profession. Why? Because our profession is based on soft skills - the human touch. You can be a specialist in using different kinds of tools and techniques but if you don't know how to communicate, than it is most likely that your project will fail. The strategy of the company is executed through projects, and having good project managers in the company is very valuable. Today most of the work is done in teams and I strongly believe that we need good servant project managers.

Q5• How can we encourage more people to pursue project management as a career?

I strongly believe that project management is one of the professions of the future. That is why I believe that it would be great to introduce project management culture to the primary school. In the year 2011, PMI Slovenia together with the international initiative of PMI, began to spread a project culture among pupils with the project we named "Projects in Bloom". PMI Slovenia volunteers who are certified professional project managers have been introducing project management learning tools to teachers to help and empower them to become more powerful project learners and leaders. In the school year of 2016/2017 around 300 pupils from 2nd to 9th grade in the Municipality of Nova Gorica learned and used project management method. On the final event, pupils and teachers presented to the public their experiences as well as exhibited project products and work results. This was an important milestone and I believe that this approach brings other great results on the kids and teachers e.g: pupils' behaviour changes. They realize that they are part of the team and that each person in the team has their role and responsibility. They feel to be a part of something important, they start to feel responsible and heard, they see results and not just grades. Even the shyest child or a troubled child felt involved and took part in the teamwork. At the end of the project, kids are recognized, and they are proud of the outcomes achieved. Project management skills are important skills for the future no matter if you are a project manager or a member of the team, and we - professional project managers - are responsible to build communities with great support and awareness for our future project managers.

Q6• What do you think are the top issues that project managers face today?

Projects today are more complex, challenging, uncertain, unpredictable and full of constant-change and this is hard to handle. Project manager role has expanded. I remember my beginnings where the success of the project was measured based on time, scope, budget and quality. The value and benefit realization were not measured. But luckily this has changed which is good for companies and customers but might give headaches to project managers because all that is now expected from them. Suddenly project managers have additional responsibility like aligning the project with strategy, gathering requirements, proving that project delivered value and benefits to the company/customer.

I believe that top issues that project managers are facing are:

- *Trust*
- *Communications*
- *Lack of clarity of goals*
- *Priorities are not clear and changing all the time*
- *Too many assumptions*
- *Roles and responsibilities are not clear*
- *Handling changes.*

Q7• Do you think there is a stereotype attached to project managers?

Unfortunately, some people still believe that project managers are bureaucrats, that this is just an administrative role.

Q8• Why is it important to celebrate international women's day?

It's important that we celebrate the international women's day because we were so long forgotten and not valued. It is important to remember all women that had an important role in the past to bring us the freedom that we have today (at least in many countries) and even more important to support all women around the world that are still fighting for their freedom. Still today we are not equal to men on so many aspects, and we need to change this. We need to raise our kids so that they will respect both genders because each of us is a human being and deserves to be treated with respect and dignity.

Q9• On international women' s day, what is the most important message you offer to project management professionals ?

In today's world, we should cherish each other and work together as one big family, equal to all genders. We need to allow ourselves to be what we are and help each other. We need each other, there is no one worthier then the other person or gender. Let's become just one big supportive family.

Alenka Gruden

Alenka Gruden, PMP®, PMO-CP® is a recognized practitioner of project and program management. She has more than 20 years of experience in the private and public sectors as a project manager, consultant, mentor and trainer. She has been serving in different industries like telecommunications, postal sector, banks, utilities, government, IT, training institutions and more. She is trustworthy, dedicated and professional. She likes to help and support people, build good relationships in the team and staying focused on achieving results within agreed deadlines, agreed quality, scope and value to the customer. She also successfully delivered several training programs in project management field. For the last five years, she has been working as an independent consultant, project manager, mentor, and trainer. She is also an international speaker. One of her personal goals is to help people to implement servant leadership principles in everyday life (personal and professional). She joined PMI® and the PMI® Slovenia Chapter in 2011, the same year when she became PMP® certified. In March 2016 she was elected as a President of PMI® Slovenia, Ljubljana Chapter until April 2018. Currently, she is the President of PMI® Slovenia Advisory Board. In the year 2017 she was elected to become part of the PMI® European Chapter Collaboration Implementation Team as Central Europe sub-region liaison and responsible for communication among the region 8 (2 years mandate in 2018 and 2019). In 2018 she graduated from the PMI® Leadership Institute Master Class. The same year she becomes a PMO certified practitioner. In 2019, she became the member of Silicon Valley Alliances and got Prosci Change Management practitioner certificate.

Angelica Maria Larios Arias
Mexico

Alacontec / CEO

Q1• Describe your journey as a project management professional.

I started to manage projects indirectly back in 2004; previously, I had experience as a project coordinator. However, my first experiences were challenged because I was new in the field, and I had not enough tools to manage projects properly. In 2007, I started my studies with a Diploma in Project Management. I prepared myself to present my PMP exam, and since then, I have actively involved in PM and PMI. I have run the projects since 2004 directly and indirectly, either being assigned in each project or as the head of a business unit or organisation helping others to grow.

Q2• Why did you choose to become a project management professional?

As I mentioned before, it was needed for my professional development. Coming from an IT background and involved in software development and consulting fields, projects are day to day activities. Having the responsibility to manage projects and deliver results, I needed to become professional and certified.

While I was studying and preparing myself to be certified, I realized that I was passionate about the subject and that I had the innate need to keep the flag of PMI with me wherever I go.

Q3• Have you encountered any related obstacles in advancing your career?

Yes, of course. All sorts of difficulties. Before obtaining my certification, I was randomly selected for an audit process that I had to surpass to present the exam. I had to face to be fired on two different occasions after being a project manager certified. However, being involved with PMI first with a local chapter, later at global operations as a volunteer, and continue developing my profession and my studies lead me to become an entrepreneur. So, obstacles are meant for us to grow and overpassing them offers new perspectives and values; being a project manager has been helpful in my professional and personal life.

Q4• Why is it important that more people work in the project management area?

Project managers are needed everywhere. We live in a world that is highly projectized; as a matter of fact, PMI has stated that we are in the Project Economy. People with the right knowledge and skills are the best bet if you want your project to succeed. Think about any project in your life, how much time, money, the effort you could have saved if you have had better tools? Project management is a must-have ability if you want to succeed in the current environment.

Q5• How can we encourage more people to pursue project management as a career?

I think there are three different markets.

- *Students. There is a need to create awareness in schools and programs to teach young people that there is a possibility in their future as professional development or career.*
- *Practicants. There is a considerable need to have knowledgeable and skillful certified people. The PMP certification is the most valuable in the market; we have to keep that value, showing that certification holders know what we are doing, promote the hiring of certified people and not allowing that others disqualify our profession.*
- *Organizations. Organizations need to be aware of the value of a methodology, such as project management. Include practice and learning about this and have a path for project managers to grow internally.*

Q6• What do you think are the top issues that project managers face today?

Keep the pace, our environment changes every day; the need for being agile everywhere and up to speed requires that project managers are trained and updated accordingly to what the market is asking for. Also, soft skills are needed to be developed as a project manager or as a leader; communication, negotiation, leadership are mandatory to succeed in our days.

Q7• Do you think there is a stereotype attached to project managers?

Unfortunately, yes, there are. Many people have the idea in their heads that the project managers don't do a thing, they don't have another job but instigate others or that the project manager is a kind of secretary taking notes. However, the figure of a project manager has to be positioned and evaluated in the right dimension.

Q8• Why is it important to celebrate international women's day?

International women's day had a different origin from the idea of what is nowadays. It started with the fight for the right to work under the same conditions that men, and now it is quite common to hear that the celebration is more about the qualities that a woman has. I think that it is crucial to have the recognition as a woman to have the same rights and obligations as a man. Recognize that we are equals as human beings but different in nature and that man and woman can apport to family, organisations, society, community, jobs, and so many different qualities. I think it is important to celebrate that we can both work, develop a career, have freedom, have a family, and many other rights under the same conditions.

Q9• On international women's day, what is the most important message you offer to project management professionals?

Well, I would say that we should not have a difference between male and female project managers. However, I understand and support that support groups are created to encourage and support women in Project Management. Women project managers are equally capable of leading a project, leading teams, and work one on one with sponsors and executives. Women are equally capable, as any other professional, women possess even different qualities that make us unique. We should celebrate the international women's day and every single day for the fortune of being female and free to design our future. If you choose to become a female project manager, well, just congratulations! You chose a profession that will tremendously challenge and reward you.

Angelica Maria Larios Arias

Angelica Larios, MBA, PMP, is a project manager with more than 20 years of experience in implementing software projects related to business intelligence, planning, and consolidation of financial solutions based on software applications to support the business decision process. She is the founder and CEO of ALACONTEC, an IT consulting company founded in Latin America. She has held several professional positions in private and public organisations, such as the Health Ministry in Mexico as IT director, and as a business manager for several firms in Mexico.

She holds a master's degree in business administration and a bachelor's degree in computer science from National University of Mexico (UNAM) in addition to her studies in project management and her Project Management Professional (PMP)® certification, which have helped her to consolidate her career and have a better understanding of what businesses and projects need nowadays. She is a doctoral student in strategic leadership at Regent University, VA, and currently serves on the Ethics Member Advisory Group (EMAG) that supports the PMI global operations (2019–2021). She has held other global volunteer positions such as BVAC (2016-2018) and CMAG (2013-2014).

Antje Lehmann-Benz
Germany

Antje Lehmann Training / Trainer and Coach

Q1• Describe your journey as a project management professional.

Like many people, I came to projects more by chance than by predetermination. As a university student of philology, I was looking for work outside of studying hours when a friend asked me if I wanted to join his team of externals for the IT department of a semiconductor corporation.

I stayed with this company for many years, also after having finished my studies, and was part of a team for global software roll out projects. Later, I went to other global organizations to lead IT projects which became increasingly influenced by agile approaches. As a Product Owner, I also trained colleagues, first teaching software usage and later also project management and agile frameworks. In that time, I decided to pursue the Project Management Professional certification by Project Management Institute and the Professional Scrum Master certification by Scrum.org. In the years after that, I also completed PMI Agile Certified Practitioner and Professional Product Owner.

Today, I am a full-time trainer and coach for project management and agile, and a long-time volunteer with Project Management Institute.

Q2• Why did you choose to become a project management professional?

Throughout the years, I discovered that while practical experience is important, it is also vital to know the theoretical foundations. So many people work in projects every day and feel unsure about where to look for knowledge to do their job more successfully. The knowledge is there; one just has to tap into it.

My ambition today is to help other practitioners in that regard. I am lucky to have been inspired and supported by my father and mentor Oliver F. Lehmann in this endeavor – as well as by PMI volunteering colleagues.

Q3• Have you encountered any related obstacles in advancing your career?

Yes, many. Some are the same for many project and project management professionals: It can be hard to find and apply appropriate tools and techniques sometimes. Also, some companies are less inclined than others to help employees in their journey to make their project management more professional. I had the pleasure to work for very supportive superiors, but also know the pains to report to those much less interested in the topic.

Another obstacle definitely concerns gender: As female project management professionals, it seems we have to prove twice as much that we are knowledgeable and experienced. We have the feeling we should hide the fact that we have children. This can be very tedious at times, but all the more incentive to help more women choose and develop careers in project management, then this will hopefully stop one day.

Q4• Why is it important that more people work in the project management area?

The reputation of project management is not always as good as it should be: Some people fear the disruptions that projects can bring to operations in an organization. Many people work in external projects where they have to be really apt at handling customers well, putting the income of their company at stake in case this doesn't go well. Some matrix companies want to run projects as a mere necessary evil instead of endeavoring to renew themselves and keep up with times. Project management professionals themselves often don't know what is possible through the application of professional project management. All this can be addressed by more and more professionally trained project managers in the field, who help improve the opinions people hold about us and our profession.

Q5• How can we encourage more people to pursue project management as a career?

Project management becomes more important with complex VUCA times, even if some people in movements such as the spreading of agile ideas claim the term "project" was a relic of the past (mostly in order to free themselves of the stigma that comes with the reputation described in 4. and to make projects "attractive" again). In fact, both worlds could easily be consolidated: project management helps see and successfully run projects as the unique and temporary endeavors that they are, and agile methods give us tools and techniques to do this in a very lightweight manner, that doesn't bog us down with too much administrative overhead and preemptive planning where that isn't helpful.

In the end, we all have the same goals and are one very large crowd of people who want to make the world a better place with projects. If that does not attract young professionals, I don't know what would. But they need to be told that this is what it is about.

Q6• What do you think are the top issues that project managers face today?

Like stated before, summed up and expanded by some more:

- *Lack of support for project managers in their careers and their professionalism*
- *Projects considered as a tedious necessity rather than a chance*
- *Lack of all kinds of diversity in the field of project management, imposter syndrome and underestimation of their own expertise in women and lack of support to uncover such problems*
- *Chasms and internal quarrels between approaches and ideas; detached language that makes project management seems something not so tangible and almost scary for some to get into*
- *Growing complexity: More and more contracted out and remote work, interconnected markets*
- *Lack of training and a recognition of the importance of training on the job*
- *Challenges that come with digitalization and development of AI (this also involves chances)*

Q7• Do you think there is a stereotype attached to project managers?

Companies that don't value project management that much, see project managers as unwanted disrupters who (in reality for lack of support) don't get anything done. Agile purists see them as people just holding titles, who are outdated and undesirable. People outside the field, see them as someones doing things they themselves will never be able to do ("that's too high up for me" is something I, as a trainer hear, often when I tell people about my job).

Q8• Why is it important to celebrate international women's day?

As long as there's room for improvement for women (and there undoubtedly is), it is more important than ever to celebrate everything meant to empower us. Not necessarily for us to receive flowers, although those are surely nice. But when asked what I want for Women's Day, or for Mother's Day, I would say "equal opportunity, thank you very much"!

Q9• On international women' s day, what is the most important message you offer to project management professionals?

Don't be afraid! Project management needs you, your expertise, your experience, your knowledge, both from your professional background as from your private one (just think back of how many private projects you've managed – weddings, house constructions, starting a family maybe? Someone in my seminar once said: "Life is a project").

Don't underestimate what you've done in the past – men don't underestimate their accomplishments either.

And although it's hard and I wish it wasn't necessary, you'll have to fend off remarks by colleagues who don't believe in you because of your gender.

23

If you feel alone, reach out to a network like PMI and specifically look for other women there, or to Lean In Circles or similar empowering movements. And lastly: support other women, regardless of race, origin, gender, physical ability, or age, to follow in your footsteps as determinedly as you are moving forward. If no employer can be found to help you on your path, consider self-employment. The project management profession offers some great opportunities to grow professionally and as a person.

There is still a lot to do, but we are paving the way one step at time.

Antje Lehmann
Project management and training professional with focus on Agile topics, Scrum, certifications (PMP, PMI-ACP, Scrum Master & Product Owner), Project Business Management (PBM).

Enjoying to help people and organizations improve their knowledge and their skills. Agile games and exercises included!

Also active as a volunteer for the Project Management Institute Southern Germany Chapter etc. (chapter magazine, career development consulting for project managers).

When possible, attending PMI chapter meetings, Agile Game Night / Liberating Structures meetups, and other networking events.

To her, the future of work is both digital and empathetic. Which is why she is passionate for workplace diversity and speaking up about it, too.

Carla Fair Wright
USA

Link Technologies / Project Manager

Q1• Describe your journey as a project management professional.

My journey as an IT project manager began when I was 18 years old. I was attending Boston University as a Biomedical Engineering major when family financial changes required me to drop out. After working for several years, I enlisted in the United States Air Force in order to finance my college degree through the military's financial aid program.

I trained in the US Air Force as a computer programmer and was assigned to Maxwell Air Force Base in Montgomery, Alabama. I enrolled in college night classes at Troy State University, unfortunately, engineering was not offered as an evening program. I knew I wanted to stay in the sciences, so I selected computer programming as my major. I enjoyed writing software and found I had a natural talent for computer science.

I graduated with a Bachelor of Science in Computer Science. What began as a disappointing alternative major was now something I really loved. I always enjoyed solving puzzles and problems and writing software was all about finding patterns and logic flow. Meanwhile, as a computer programmer in the military, I was also learning a great deal about leadership and team building, and I even continued night school pursuing a Masters in Personnel Management to develop my interpersonal skills.

Q2. Why did you choose to become a project management professional?

I chose to become a project manager because it seemed like a natural progression for me. After I left the military, I worked as a computer programmer, eventually becoming a technical lead. The constantly changing nature of IT was fun and exciting, but I felt I had more to offer. This was when I started to envision myself as a project manager. I got my first real project manager position in Houston, Texas working for the Houston Police Department. My military background helped me to understand the hierarchical culture of law enforcement. My technical background gave me a unique insight into computer programming and the ability to speak the language of the software developers.

As I began to invest more time in improving as a project manager, I realized that I had lots of useful information I wanted to share with other project managers and I began writing for technical journals such as Code Magazine and Reliability Magazine. Then came the opportunity to contribute to a book with Francis Taylor, a major technical publisher, and speaking engagements started coming my way. I began developing conference presentations and have spoken at international conferences in Frankfurt, London, Barcelona, and Dublin.

Q3. Have you encountered any related obstacles in advancing your career?

I faced many obstacles as a female IT project manager. In addition to gender bias and stereotyping of women in the sciences, there were also the elements of racial bias. As much as I loved Sheryl Samberg's "Lean In" it didn't address the unique circumstances for women of color who face a different type of systematic barriers. My competency was often challenged, despite having several degrees, certifications, and proven experience. I was passed over for promotions and watched as important or high visibility projects were assigned to male peers.

As with any challenge the key to success is through knowledge and action. I was fortunate to have a strong support group. Recruited into the Society of Women Engineers (SWE) as a college freshman I received solid professional advice from senior women, who had navigated the heavily male dominated field of engineering with careers that spanned decades. The organization provided a place to build lasting friendships and great mentorships.

Q4• Why is it important that more people work in the project management area?

There is a global shortage of project management professionals. According to a recent article in CIO magazine, it is putting many businesses at a competitive disadvantage. The Project Management Institute (PMI) estimated that "the talent gap could result in a potential loss of some $207.9 billion in GDP through 2027".

Q5• How can we encourage more people to pursue project management as a career?

Recruiting talent into the project management career requires broadening the pool of talent. One of the solutions in science, technology, engineering and mathematics or STEM was to build a pipeline of talent. The process starts by reaching out to a younger audience to build awareness of the profession through educational programs. The goal is to encourage project management as a career choice early on, so that there is a constant flow of talent into the field.

Q6•   What do you think are the top issues that project managers face today?

Power stress is the top issue in project management today. It is a silent health issue that results from the constant exercise of influence and sense of responsibility felt in leadership positions. This is a key symptom of the "Sacrifice Syndrome". According to Richard Boyatzis and Annie McKee, writers of "Resonant Leadership", Sacrifice Syndrome can occur over time because of a number of factors, including pressure to get results, heavy responsibilities, the perpetual need to influence people and feelings of loneliness.

Q7•   Do you think there is a stereotype attached to project managers?

Yes, I believe there is definitely a stereotype for project managers. Because the project manager's job is to stay focused on the financials, planning, and quality. A certain image has formed around the profession. Project managers are often seen as structured, meeting-happy, rigid, and task focused.

Q8•   Why is it important to celebrate international women's day?

It is important to celebrate IWD because gender equality is still only a dream for our daughters.

Q9•   On international women' s day, what is the most important message you offer to project management professionals?

The project management professional is a leader and as leaders, we should always aspire to treat all with fairness and respect.

Carla Fair Wright

Carla Fair-Wright has been involved in software development and project management for more than 20 years and has worked in oil and gas, engineering, manufacturing, law enforcement, and education. She is a Software Engineer, Project Management and Change Management Specialist.

An award-winning international speaker and author on the subject of project management, she has appeared on Terri Craig Radio Show, and Business Makers Small Business Network Show and has been featured in the National Society of Black Engineers (NSBE) magazine, Maintenance Technology, STEMINST, and Code Magazine. Her most recently conducted lectures on leadership were at the 2019 Project Management Institute (PMI) conference in Dublin, 2016 and 2015 Project Management Institute (PMI) Global conferences in Barcelona and London, Project Management Institute-Frankfurt, and the University of Houston's Asian Affairs department. Carla is the chapter author of two books, 'Encyclopedia of Energy Engineering and Technology' and 'Case Studies and Applications of Web-Based Energy Information and Control Systems'.

A member of the Society of Women Engineers since 2007, Carla has held several board offices both local and national. She is the past President of Society of Women Engineers (Houston) and a recipient of the 2014 Regional Emerging Leader award. She was twice awarded Cameron's Technical Publication and Presentation Award for her published books and conference presentations. As a community volunteer, Carla has served in many capacities over the years. In 2010, she was appointed by former Mayor White as a Commissioner on Houston City Buildings and Standards board and has worked closely with disadvantaged teens in low-income schools, as part of the Project Hope organization.

Cecilia Boggi
Argentina

activePMO / Founder and Executive Director

Q1• Describe your journey as a project management professional.

Sometimes unexpected things happen to us. In my case, after working 20 years in software development and information technology projects, initially as part of the team, and then leading projects, I had the bad luck of becoming unemployed at a time when my country, Argentina, was going through a severe economic crisis.

That bad luck became a great opportunity, since given the difficulty of finding another job, I decided to take the time for training and thus came the idea of preparing for the Project Management Professional (PMP) certification and obtaining this prestigious credential, which at that time was not very well-known in my country.

From that unwanted situation, I found the right moment for my professional development and after that, my life changed forever, not only professionally, but also personally. Obtaining the PMP credential and approaching PMI opened doors for me, both in Argentina and throughout Latin America and allowed me to meet excellent people from all over the world.

Q2• Why did you choose to become a project management professional?

I must say, to be honest, that I did not choose to become a project manager, instead it was naturally, as a journey in my professional career. I started writing code, then I went on to perform the functional analysis and lead the development team and then lead the entire project and finally I had the opportunity to implement and manage the Project Management Office (PMO) of a Software Factory. Currently, I have my own company providing consulting services for organizations to design and improve their PMOs and practices of projects, programs and portfolios management.

Having had the PMP certification was for me an important differential in my career. As an example, I can mention that in 2004 I started working as a Project Manager in an important international company based in Spain and when presenting the certificate of my PMP credential, my boss informed me that I was the only project management professional certified in that company of more than 6000 employees in various countries of the world. Today, that organization is one of those that supports Project Management Institute (PMI) worldwide and strongly promotes PMP certification.

Q3• Have you encountered any related obstacles in advancing your career?

I cannot say that I have encountered obstacles in my career as a project manager, since, on the contrary, owning the PMP® credential allowed me to take advantage of interesting opportunities and access leadership positions.

However, I believe that what gave me this credential the most was the security and confidence to enforce my opinion with the knowledge authority and the support of thousands of project managers who recommend the good practices of the PMBOK Guide®. I think this confidence was decisive in my professional career.

Q4• Why is it important that more people work in the project management area?

We are experiencing the project revolution, the world is being driven by projects and organizations are recognizing that, to carry out the strategies that allow them to endure in an increasingly dynamic, uncertain and competitive market, they must execute projects. That is why project management is one of the fastest growing professions in today's world and that the need for project managers with the right skills are being highly valued globally. Those organizations that do not have these professionals have difficulties in achieving their goals and making their initiatives reality. Having more professional project managers, with the appropriate skills, improves the resource utilization efficiency in projects.If we consider companies in private sector, they will obtain greater profits and will be able to provide more jobs.
In parallel, thinking of the state agencies, efficiency in projects translates into greater benefits for the communities and less taxes for citizens and companies.Briefing, having more talented project managers is beneficial in all areas.

Q5• How can we encourage more people to pursue project management as a career?

We cannot love what we don't know. If we want more people approaching and embracing project management as a professional career, we need to disseminate it. In this sense, as a volunteer of the Board of Directors of PMI Buenos Aires, Argentina Chapter initially, and then as a PMI Mentor in Latin America I tried to spread this profession both among university students who would surely participate in projects in their professional life, as well as in organizations and public organizations that developed projects intuitively, without knowing the good practices recommended by the community of global project managers, through the PMBOK Guide®.

Currently, as a professor of the Master in Educational Institutions Management and the Bachelor of Educational Organization and Management of the Austral University of Buenos Aires, Argentina, I have the opportunity to convey the importance of properly managing projects to a totally new audience for me, as so are the directors of schools and educational institutions of initial and middle level. My desire is that these people embrace project management, apply it to their projects and transmit it to their students, to generate interest in children and young people.

Q6· What do you think are the top issues that project managers face today?

I think that the biggest challenges of today's project managers are related to the new skills they must acquire to continue being relevant in a world of vertiginous changes. It is required to be updated with respect to technological advances, such as Big Data, internet of things, artificial intelligence, in addition to the dynamism of the markets and the increasingly demanding requirements of customers and consumers, sustainability, and so on.

Today, professionals who want to continue giving value to their organizations have to be constantly updated in global trends.

On the other hand, more and more projects have strong pressures to reduce deadlines and costs in order to deliver products to the market before their competitors.

All this means that world require project managers with knowledge of the business and industry, a leadership style that promote continuously innovation, learning and improving from their teams.

Q7• Do you think there is a stereotype attached to project managers?

According to studies conducted by the Project Management Institute (PMI), it is estimated that only about 30% of the world's project managers are women.

On the other hand, the areas or industries that have the greatest impact on project management tend to be predominantly masculine, for example, the construction, software and the information technology industries.

As well as there is a stereotype of leader with male traits and characteristics, it seems that the project manager model also follows those parameters.

However, more and more, organizations are perceiving that women can contribute a lot to projects and businesses, with their transformational, collaborative and empathic leadership style.

Recently, Goldman Sachs CEO, David Solomon, announced a new regulation that companies must have at least one woman on the board or will not make the companies public, and that they should have two women on the board by 2021, since the initial public offerings of companies in the United States with at least one female director on their boards performed "significantly better" compared to those that did not.

Source: https://edition.cnn.com/2020/01/23/investing/goldman-sachs-ipo-diversity/index.html

Q8• Why is it important to celebrate international women's day?

International Women's Day is an opportunity to remind those women who fought and gave their lives for greater inclusion in the labor market.

At present, the workforce is practically matched in terms of the number of women and men, however, if we look at leadership roles, equity is totally lost.

Studies show that only 5 to 6% of the CEO positions of the most recognized companies are held by women, reaching approximately 25% when all leading line management positions are included, those that begin with the letter "C", such as CFO, CIO, COO, etc.

In the case of project managers, as I stated before, there is also a big gap.

International Women's Day helps the world become aware of these important gaps and join forces to reduce them all together.

Q9•   On international women' s day, what is the most important message you offer to project management professionals?

My message for project management professionals, both women and men, is to remember that through projects we are changing something in the world, with our example we can influence many young people and their professional decisions.

Let us be a model for young people, women and men, who respect each other, who respect diversity and value differences.

Together we will make a more intense change, and the world needs it.

Cecilia Boggi

Graduated in Systems Analysis from Universidad de Buenos Aires Argentina, Executive MBA at Universidad Francisco de Vitoria, Spain, Business Management Program at Universidad del CEMA. Certified Project Management Professional PMP, PMI-ACP, Certified Scrum Master, Certified PMO-CP, Certified Leadership Facilitator in SDI, Toastmasters Competent Communicator, Professional Executive Coach and Graduated from PMI Leadership Institute Master Class in 2012.

More than 30 years of experience in leading software development projects, organizational processes projects, Project Management Offices implementation and Consulting, both in the private and public sectors, in Argentina, Chile, Bolivia, Ecuador, other countries in Latin America and Spain.

Founder and Executive Director of activePMO, a Consulting and Training company specialized in Leadership and Project Management skills.

Professor of international Universities and Business Schools. International speaker at conferences in Latin America and North America.

Instructor at Inter-American Development Bank (IDB), teaching Leadership courses for Project Management to the IDB-financed project teams in several Latin American countries, since 2014.

Author of the book "Induction to Project Management" in 2020, co-author of the books "Innovation and Strategic Project Management" in 2013 and "Best Management Practices. Volume II" in 2019, author of "ANNEX B - Scrum", of the book "Agile Project Management" by Pablo Lledó in 2012.

Author of several articles on Project Management and Leadership and correspondent of Argentina, for the monthly publication PM World Journal between 2013 and 2019. www.pmworldjournal.net

PMI Member and Volunteer since 2002, President of PMI Buenos Aires Argentina Chapter in 2011, PMI Region Mentor for Southern Latin America since 2014 to 2017.

Leader of Chapter 9-Project Human Resources Management Team of the PMBOK® 5th Edition update content team, 2010-2012.

Currently, Leader of the Community of Interest "Women in Project Management Leadership" in PMI Buenos Aires Argentina Chapter and facilitator of the WiPM Leadership Blog at www.projectmanagement.com.

Claude El Nakhel Khalil (Dr.)
Lebanon

ALGORITHM SAL Pharmaceutical Manufacturers / Technical services and Product Development Manager

Q1• Describe your journey as a project management professional.

My journey started as a project manager in a pharmaceutical manufacturing environment. The role was exclusively associated with the production part of the service, being a Production Manager with a set of pharmaceutical skills that I gained throughout my career as a pharmacist.

The role of a project manager was new. I had to prove that as much as my role was important in "What we deliver "and "When we deliver", the role of a project manager is equally important in the "How we deliver" part of the operation, in building Quality systems, and positive experience for all stakeholders.

Being professional, always delivering what is planned and promised, in terms of quality, cost-effectiveness, in an open communication and regulated environment, building partnership relations with authorities and principals. For these competencies are well-known and frequently described as the characteristics of a good project manager.

But the role of the project manager in health care experience does not start with the project handoff and ends with the delivery.

I was the project manager who often guided major stakeholders and the team members to make the journey as smooth as possible; often trying to improve with technology, by automating some of the tasks, by providing the organization where I work with an insight into project management processes and by making the processes more transparent.

I have put my knowledge and experience to assess what lies ahead at the initial stages of the project – identify the risks and issues that may emerge during the project, and I was often involved deeply in the decision-making process.

I have learned that precision, timeliness and appropriateness of a project manager's communication showing respect for all stakeholders are the most important aspects of project management.

I mostly enjoy giving back to the community, by mentoring and teaching. My volunteering journey with PMI added a value to my expertise; by giving back I enjoyed a lifetime learning experience.

Q2• Why did you choose to become a project management professional?

All started by chance. I was assigned a small project based on my technical skills in the pharmaceutical industry. From there, I dived into a world of standards, guidelines, resources, and competencies through designing and executing master project plans, then to discover PMP certification and the importance of volunteering with PMI, where I was lucky to find my passion, and so a new journey of self-development and giving back has begun.

Q3• Have you encountered any related obstacles in advancing your career?

The major obstacle I have usually encountered is the lack of clear communication, mainly navigating through different communication styles.

Prioritization of communication in a project can be an obstacle in a multi-cultural environment. I sometimes have struggled with systems that make it a challenge to complete a task because of a red tape: Staff attitudes and the bureaucracy that resist to change.

Q4• Why is it important that more people work in the project management area?

While project management has become a popular career, individuals in any different role can benefit from project management tools and techniques to set and achieve their key business goals. Adopting project management techniques can lead to increase team's productivity and focus on key objectives driving the team to achieve success.

Q5• How can we encourage more people to pursue project management as a career?

Project management provides many different benefits. It is a career path that will allow professionals to feel fulfilled, offering stability and growth.

Working as project manager professional is proved to enhance the professional life. Practitioners feel challenged and stimulated in a position where they can contribute in changing global economy. For example, the healthcare sector has shown the need for more project managers due to continuously changing regulations, and increasing competition.

Being a project manager contributes to adding value to the community and organizations, creating a value, and most importantly ensuring innovation and global growth.

Q6• What do you think are the top issues that project managers face today?

The most challenging aspects of project manager roles can be summarized in handling difficult projects and obtaining positive results. In order to balance all key elements of a complex project, a project manager has to work hard on a daily basis. One of the most common challenges a project manager has to face usually regards corporate internal issues. Most of the time, these issues can be related to having poorly defined goals of an organization, leading to unclear requirements and subsequent changes during execution.

Furthermore, some projects can be challenging and can demand a certain level of knowledge and expertise.Therefore, a project manager has to possess an array of skills surrounding communication, decision-making, delegation, and risk-taking.

Not to mention that lack of accountability, responsibility, and quality can halt the project and leave the project manager in a confusing situation.

Q7• Do you think there is a stereotype attached to project managers?

The project manager role is often inaccurately interpreted. Because some organizations have different definitions of project management, there is sometimes a lack of clarity around the role, especially for non-project management professionals.

One of the most stereotypical expectations attached to project managers is being the "meeting note taker" or "meeting organizer". There is another misconception that the project manager is the only team member who should care about the "budget".

Q8• Why is it important to celebrate international women's day?

International Women's Day continues to be a powerful platform that unifies tenacity, and drives action for gender parity, while celebrating social, cultural, economic, and political achievements of women worldwide.

The values that guide International Women's Day provide direction to deeply understand and celebrate women's achievements. Looking back to look forward, values have guided women's campaigning for action and recognition.

The values like Justice, Dignity, Hope, Equality, Collaboration, Tenacity, Appreciation, Respect, Empathy, and most importantly Forgiveness are deeply needed to achieve fairness and peace during tumultuous times.

Q9• On international women' s day, what is the most important message you offer to project management professionals?

Supporting women's ability to succeed and advance in Project Economy will definitely lead to healthy and productive households, growing and successful businesses, and most importantly the well-being of our nations worldwide.

Claude El Nakhel

Dr. Claude El Nakhel is an accomplished and well-seasoned pharmacist specialized in the pharmaceutical industrial field.

She received her doctorate D 'exercises in pharmacy from Saint Joseph University, Beirut, and her MBA from Newport University California- Beirut Affiliation. In addition to her professional career in pharmaceutical industry, Dr. El Nakhel is a teacher of Project management at different reputable Universities in Lebanon- graduate programs.

Dr. El Nakhel was elected President of PMI Lebanon chapter and has contributed to the growth of the Project management community in her region.

Deena Gordon Parla
USA

Global Business Management Consultants / Director

Q1• Describe your journey as a project management professional.

My career began as laptop computers, local area networks, and email were being integrated into the professional workplace. I was hired as a programmer/analyst for a large consulting firm in Washington, D.C. Information technology and communications (ICT) were rapidly being introduced to enable both private and public sector organizations streamline operational processes. The business case was driven by cost and time savings from the re-engineered and technology-enabled business processes.

During those early years, I discovered that many ICT solution projects had significant risks for failure, including:

- *Project manager role was loosely defined, with key responsibilities often defaulting to the technical or functional leads who did not have PM skills training.*
- *Mismatch of technology capability and business requirements at the detailed specifications level.*

- *Executive sponsor's lack of commitment to resolving resource conflicts or regularly communicating why the IT solution/change to operational processes was important.*
- *Misperception that IT solution users would accept changes to their daily business processes.*

To reduce these risks, I took on additional team leadership roles as a bridge between the IT solution's business customers and the technical specialists, as well as invested time for team building and project stakeholder communications.

A decade later, the introduction of web-based e-commerce solutions and agile development approaches enabled businesses and IT project teams to more easily collaborate and shorten delivery time frames. As a project leader, in-depth understanding of operational business processes and the ability to communicate how the project solution aligns with business strategy became even more important than technical expertise. This was true regardless of the industry or global region I worked in.

Since then, my professional journey has evolved into program management and PMO roles, as emphasis has shifted from operational to strategic transformation programs of increasing complexity.

Q2· Why did you choose to become a project management professional?
During the first half of my career, professional PM roles were not common, especially for recent computer science degree graduates. Often there were only two career paths– technical or functional. I enjoyed problem solving through technology, but from a more

strategic, broader organizational perspective. After joining the Project Management Institute (PMI) in 1999, I found opportunities to network and volunteer with PMs in different stages of their career. It validated my decision to focus on project management professionally. It is incredibly rewarding to engage with strategic projects/programs, as successful execution requires ongoing alignment with business strategy while delivering measurable value to an organization.

Q3• Have you encountered any related obstacles in advancing your career?

Several challenges come to mind:

1. *When project success was determined by a yes/no answer to "was it on time" and "was it within budget", rather than assessing value realized by the business for the resources invested.*

2. *Success factors tied to soft skills were not as valued. For example:*
   - *Focus on team dynamics – build cohesion, alignment and foster innovation by bridging across cultures and geographically dispersed organizational units.*
   - *Integrate change management activities into the project scope.*
   - *Maintain alignment through effective communication with the project team and stakeholders.*

   As a result, team building and stakeholder communications tasks were the first to be "trimmed" to shorten project schedules. Also, soft skills were not consistently given the same priority for talent development.

3. *Leading projects in highly matrixed organizations adds layers of complexity:*

- *Confusion or overlapping roles and responsibilities across the project (ie. product manager, requirements analyst, change manager, project manager, functional lead, etc.).*
- *Increased focus on stakeholder management activities.*
- *Inconsistent understanding of the project manager role by project stakeholders.*

Fortunately, as organizational PM maturity increases across organizations globally, the impact of these obstacles has decreased.

Q4• Why is it important that more people work in the project management area?

PMI defines "The Project Economy" as one in which people have the skills and capabilities they need to turn ideas into reality. It is where organizations deliver value to stakeholders through successful completion of projects, delivery of products, and alignment to value streams. And all of these initiatives deliver financial and societal value. (https://www.pmi.org/the-project-economy)

This means that the environment we deliver projects, continues to grow more complex and global. There is continuous demand for PM talent with a global citizens mindset; adapt at blending leadership skills (inspire, collaborate, communicate), business acumen, and technical knowledge.

Becoming a project management professional adapted to the Project Economy provides an opportunity to lead multi-cultural project teams and develop beyond technical skills. PMs with essential soft-skills, (e.g. flexibility, open-mindedness, communication, empathy) lead project teams to innovate and adapt to new or unfamiliar work environments, reflect unique cultural considerations, as well as remain aligned across different geographic time-zones and communication preferences.

Q5• How can we encourage more people to pursue project management as a career?

Practically speaking, PM skills are transferable across industries and organizational roles. It is an investment that professionals can build upon throughout their careers.

As project professionals take on larger, more complex strategic initiatives with increased resources and responsibilities, the PM skillset is more closely aligned than ever with the C-suite. With a higher cost in terms of resources and market position lost when projects fail, successful project leaders are those with the experience and flexibility to deliver projects at the same pace as the organization is changing. This is in addition to the strong leadership and cross-cultural communication skills needed to adapt and thrive in an increasingly complex, global environment.

PMs, therefore, are becoming more qualified than ever to lead at higher levels of management. We are already seeing this trend in the IT sector with the CIO role, which is being filled by professionals with direct experience in leading technology project teams. Additionally, C-Level managers with experience successfully delivering complex strategic initiatives are well suited to fill project/program Executive Sponsor roles.

Q6• What do you think are the top issues that project managers face today?

Organizations are under increasing pressure to adapt quickly to the impacts and fast pace of technology disruption. Project management professionals are on the front line of the change, responsible for executing strategy and delivering value to the organization via complex, highly visible projects. This leaves little time for PM professionals to receive training on the latest digital (e.g. data science, cyber-security, privacy, AI) and collaborative leadership skillsets. Project economy-ready PM professionals are needed by organizations. Otherwise, they will not be agile enough to compete and survive the impact of technology disruption.

Q7• Do you think there is a stereotype attached to project managers?

Yes, and unfortunately negative stereotypes arise when stakeholder(s) do not see the benefit of a project management process(es), such as a periodic review of the risk register, report progress against baseline schedule, etc. On several occasions I heard, "Here comes the project management police!" when I entered a conference room for a project performance review. Although we were streamlining our PM practices, the perception that project managers add an administrative burden to projects for technical/functional project team members remained.

Another stereotype is the perception the project managent roles are only operational, not strategic. Gaps between strategy and execution result in missed opportunities, increased costs and failure to execute. Projects are the bridge between the two, and thus project management has an important, strategic role in every organization.

Q8• Why is it important to celebrate international women's day?

In 1975, the United Nations began celebrating International Women's Day, annually, on 8 March. It is a global day celebrating the social, economic, cultural and political achievements of women. The day also marks a call to action for accelerating women's equality. (https://www.internationalwomensday.com/Theme)

International organizations and development organizations worldwide fund projects to achieve the UN's 2030 Agenda for Sustainable Development and its 17 Sustainable Development Goals(SDG). SDG 5 is "Achieve gender equality and empower all women and girls".

Celebrating International Women's Day provides global context for the efforts of international development project managers: when women are empowered, the world is in a much stronger position to address social, economic and environmental challenges world-wide.

Q9• On international women' s day, what is the most important message you offer to project management professionals?

"The International Women's Day 2020 campaign theme is drawn from a notion of 'Collective Individualism'. We are all parts of a whole. Our individual actions, conversations, behaviors and mindsets can have an impact on our larger society. Collectively, we can make change happen. Collectively, we can each help to create a gender equal world". (https://www.internationalwomensday.com/Theme)

When project teams are inspired by "Collective Individualism", they embrace diversity of ideas and the best of everyone's individual capability. Through this spirit of "collective action & shared responsibility", projects can bring positive, innovative, and sustainable change to our world.

Deena Gordon Parla
Ms. Deena Gordon Parla, PMP, has extensive leadership experience in strategy development, business transformation, and

project/program/portfolio management, primarily in the ICT, pharmaceutical, R&D, energy and defense industries. This includes delivery of projects for global multi-national corporations, governmental and not-for-profit organizations in North America and EMEA who are seeking to close the gap between strategy and execution.

Recent strategic transformation engagements include:
Strategy implementation framework for Zenith Quest Corporation, Raytheon's defense and information security solutions partner for Turkey,
PMO framework for EMEA-wide Sales transformation initiative,
Program assurance services to organizations undertaking strategic mergers/acquisitions.

Ms. Gordon Parla is an adjunct instructor for project management at the Middle Eastern Technical University in Turkey. Previously at Booze & Co, she worked with CXO level clientele to transform e-business strategies into e-solutions that delivered operational savings and increased market share. She has also served as Secretary, Board of Directors, for the bi-national Turkish American Association-Ankara.

Ms. Gordon Parla has served PMI as a volunteer leader since 2004. While on the PMI International Board of Directors (2013-2016), she served as Chair of the Strategy Development and Oversight Committee, responsible for guiding the PMI Board's strategic dialogue and planning. She has also worked on strategic initiatives for chapters worldwide, including improved chapter governance processes, reporting, and roll out of the chapter conflict resolution framework.

*Ms. Gordon Parla is a keynote speaker at PM conferences and PMI®
Leadership Institute Meetings globally. She graduated from the
invitation only, PMI® Leadership Institute Master Class in 2007*

Deanna Landers
USA

Charter Communications / Director (Program Management)

Q1•   Describe your journey as a project management professional.

My career started with a software development focus. In the late 1980s I was a computer programmer of operating systems, and applications taking advantage of new technology.

Back then, I wasn't aware of a profession called project management, but I was caught up in the common approach of leadership selection: If you were good at what you did, you were promoted to manage people who do what you did well. And from there you learned on the job, sometimes with advice from others but not always.

My first job leading a team of software developers resulted in a strong lesson about project management. I was still in college, working for a startup company, managing a team in the office, plus a contractor who worked outside the office. The contractor seemed reluctant to share information beyond the fact that "all is on track", even when I pushed him for details. When I finally shared my concern with my boss, she told me that I needed to look at his code to make sure that he did what he said, and I was horrified! I was essentially going to tell this man who was over twice my age, that I didn't trust him and needed to validate the quality of his work. But I worked up the courage to communicate my desire to understand his work status fully, and when I didn't back down, and told him that he'd need to show me his code, or we'd have to let him go, he opened his briefcase and brought out a yellow pad of paper with writing on it. My heart sank - after a couple of months, he had no code in a system, just ideas on paper. As I spent the next few weeks working day and night to complete the work the contractor hadn't completed, I was constantly reminded of how important milestone reviews are!

Q2• Why did you choose to become a project management professional?

When I became a project manager, project management was considered the "accidental profession". People didn't typically strive to enter the profession, but ended up in it through their foray into leadership, typically people and project leadership. Since I've always enjoyed novel activities, and a career in project management allowed for involvement in such a diversity of endeavors, it was an obvious fit.

Q3• Have you encountered any related obstacles in advancing your career?

The largest obstacle that I have encountered to advancing in my career was the fact that for a long while, I didn't pay attention to office politics. I worked hard and did a good job and figured that I would be rewarded and recognized appropriately. My recognition and advancement were so much greater when I started paying attention to the unwritten and unstated goals, policies, alliances, conflicts and values in the workplace. Once this new layer of knowledge was revealed, I understood my environment much better and could behave in a manner more consistent with what the culture and leadership valued.

Q4• Why is it important that more people work in the project management area?

Millions of people work in the project management profession, and even more are working in the periphery, using some project management skills or techniques, but focusing on a different discipline, like engineering or accounting. Being considered within a particular profession has certain advantages, like speaking a common language and sharing best practices along with other advantages kinship and community.

Being involved with the professional association of PMI helped me stay on top of the issues in the profession and in business, the solutions, the latest tools and techniques, and develop relationships that have lasted through the decades. These connections I made through the profession allowed me to recognize the need for project management in the humanitarian sector and the opportunity we had to address that need, leading to the foundation of Project Managers Without Borders.

Q5• How can we encourage more people to pursue project management as a career?

We could encourage more people to pursue project management as a career by helping them understand that projects are the vehicle through which our society implements strategic initiatives, provides disaster or humanitarian relief efforts, or brings any innovation to fruition. The contributions we can make to the economy, humanity, technology and the world through project management are tremendously rewarding, and endless. In addition, the nature of projects is that they are temporary, so the work is never mundane, or repetitive. Project managers may use the same tools or templates between projects, but the business value being provided and the challenges of each project are unique.

Q6• What do you think are the top issues that project managers face today?

Business today is very demanding, requiring faster results more often. Many organizations are using, dabbling in or transitioning to an agile approach, and if project managers don't transition at the same time, their roles may become obsolete. This could be seen as an issue, but it's better to consider it an opportunity – to step forward and be an essential part of the way the organization delivers its value. Maintaining career growth and relevance is something that project managers need to stay focused on, in order to be engaged in a rewarding career.

Q7• Do you think there is a stereotype attached to project managers?

Within the project management profession, I've worked in many industries and for many companies. The least mature of the organizations from a project management perspective perceive project managers as administrators, those who set up meetings, take notes, and provide reminders for upcoming milestones. They are missing the significant value that project managers can provide, and the truly unfortunate aspect is that this may be propagated by the project managers themselves, and their own leadership as well. By behaving in a way that supports this notion, it is supported. Instead, project managers need to challenge the existing stereotypes in their organizations by driving projects to completion, realizing business benefits, and communicating widely those benefits.

Q8• Why is it important to celebrate international women's day?

International Women's Day focuses on the support of equality in our world. On this day and every day, we as individuals can and should choose to defy and contest stereotypes, fight bias, and renounce discrimination, all in the pursuit of equality. Discrimination against any people is not just unethical, but also ignorant, since so much can be gained from diversity in its many forms. Equality is not a women's issue, but a humanity issue and a business issue.

Q9• On international women' s day, what is the most important message you offer to project management professionals?

Don't put too much creed in what you believe or even have been told you "should" do.

You are unique, and can certainly take into account the opinions of others, but realize that they are just that: opinions. Your distinctive perspective may be just what is needed to create a wildly refreshing new product, to develop an inspirational approach to address your organization's challenges, or to take a broader and thoughtful look at strategic options. Nobody else has a right to limit your contributions or direction, and the only way that limitation occurs is if you let it. Don't.

Deanna Landers

Deanna Landers is Director of Program Management at Charter Communications, responsible for leading a team to deliver successful network implementation, and improving the maturity and effectiveness of project, program and portfolio management. Prior to working for Charter, she was with IBM for 11 years, contributing to their award-winning Project Management Center of Excellence through the Project Management Curriculum Steering Committee and the Project

Management Certification Board, as well as delivering a $350M portfolio of projects.

She also served on the boards of IEEE Smart Village, Metro Denver PM Education Foundation, PMI Mile Hi Chapter, and for 6 years on the international board of directors of the Project Management Institute (PMI), leading the board as Chair in 2013. She is the Founder of Project Managers Without Borders (PMWB), a nonprofit organization that engages the global project management community through collaborative and sustainable projects that make a positive difference in the world. PMWB partners with other humanitarian organizations, helping them deliver their projects more efficiently and effectively, to support communities in need. She also currently serves on the Project Management Advisory Board at the University of Denver, University College.

Diana Milena Ramirez Leon

Colombia

SEITON / Managing Partner

PMI Bogotá Colombia Chapter / Vice President of Government Politics

Q1• Describe your journey as a project management professional.

I think that all my life has been based on projects, I don't really like routine activities and I have great potential to conceive, and launch new initiatives, after that, when the repetitive operation begins, I prefer to look for new challenges. I studied an engineering branch where the permanent is project management.

Once I finished my undergraduate career, I was working in a company where I learned practices in quality management and project management, so I decided to do more research and specialize in integrated management systems. There I saw for the first time a subject dedicated to project management, and this caught my attention a lot, because; although I was always leading or being part of a project team, after learning about the subject, I understood that these could be managed better. Then, years later, I decided to do a Masters in project management and become certified as PMP.

The moment I was doing the Master's Degree I realized that perhaps the most important area of knowledge of any project; is the management of stakeholders, because to the extent that you get all people to connect with the objective of the project and feel part of this, success is assured.

Today, I deeply believe in organizational management as the cornerstone and the fundamental basis for achieving a good project management and for achieving the expected results.

Q2• Why did you choose to become a project management professional?

Well, that is a long story. My professional training is topographic engineering and although the development of technical skills in my field of action was very good, the exercise of the profession that precisely responds to a logic by projects, led me to identify the need to learn more about topics of management and develop managerial skills, as I was advancing in my professional career. Today I am a teacher and consultant in project management and I love it.

Q3• Have you encountered any related obstacles in advancing your career?

Yes, mainly in public organizations in my country. The truth is that I developed most of my professional career in the public sector and unfortunately, Colombia suffers from good practices in project management in the public sphere, this causes projects to have serious problems on the entire horizon: from its definition, study of feasibility and of course in the management of the project and operation. I believe that there is a great opportunity to make projects aiming at the social and economic development of the country better and more efficient.

Q4• Why is it important that more people work in the project management area?

I consider it a wonderful experience that allows you to get to know different industries, make things happen in an organized way and be an agent of transformation and permanent development in any organization and in the world. Finally, projects are the driving force that give life to companies.

Q5• How can we encourage more people to pursue project management as a career?

I think the most important thing is to start with cross-cutting skills development components from basic education in children and other nuclei in high school and undergraduate careers. Currently, at least in my country the level of training in project management is mostly focused on postgraduate programs; specializations, masters and doctorates, this makes professionals very good in their technical skills but have limitations in management skills of effectively and efficiently directing a project.

Q6• What do you think are the top issues that project managers face today?

We are currently in a world that is moving very fast and I believe that traditional management or cascade models should be complementary with hybrid schemes that include agile practices, which have certainly taken a lot of strength considering the high level of uncertainty to define the scope of projects. Also today organizations face challenges of digital transformation and process automation. Of course, there are still industries that can manage their projects with traditional management, but it is clear that a hybrid model may have a better response to react quickly to the needs of markets and end customers.

Particularly, I believe that there is a deep work in the models of organizational management that allow the development of potential of the team members, to increase their participation as well as the understanding and the commitment of people with the project.

Q7• Do you think there is a stereotype attached to project managers?

Perhaps yes, the traditional model for companies that do not know the role of the project manager has made some companies consider that project manager's role instead of facilitating the execution of the project, makes it even more complex, by implementing too many procedures that inhibit flexibility of the teams and this cause them perceived as bureaucratic models. It happened a lot with the evolution of PMOs. However, I believe that in companies where there are better levels of maturity in project management, this stereotype has been overcome, and as I mentioned before, the inclusion of agile practices in project management has allowed us to rethink rigid and bureaucratic schemes for management of these.

Q8• Why is it important to celebrate international women's day?

Because women are the creative energy that moves the world, we are on earth because a woman gave us life. It is important to value and vindicate the role of women as the fundamental axis of the family and society. There is a very successful phrase out there that indicates "what is behind every great man there is a great woman who supports him".

Q9• On international women' s day, what is the most important message you offer to project management professionals?

The sum of the two energies: creative on the part of the woman and of action on the part of the man are the perfect synergy to move the world. I believe that the participation and collaboration of these two roles allows us to have a better vision of challenges we face as society. I do not believe in any way that any of the genders; feminine, or masculine are more important to each other. But I strongly believe that the differences between them are complementary and that they make this profession a better exercise. In that logic it is pertinent to claim the role of women with an equitable remuneration in the salary levels offered in the profession.

Diana Milena Ramirez Leon

I was born in Bogotá Colombia in 1979. The taste for the study inherited from my lawyer mother, who insisted on the importance of preparing, being an ethical person and a good professional.

I graduated as a technical bachelor in natural sciences, in 1995, in a public institution in Bogotá as a topographic engineer.

At 20, I became the mother of a son who is a great source of inspiration, being a mother changes your life and is one of the most complex, challenging but happiest projects that anyone can experience.

I worked as an engineer in many public companies in my country and I always had the precept that things can be done better. In the public sector in Colombia things do not work as well as in private companies.

In 2010, I graduated from a specialization in integrated management systems in Environmental Quality and Occupational Health and Safety. In 2016, I finished my Master's degree in project management.

I have been a teacher since 2011, and my current professional profile is as an agile coach. Trainer, consultant and auditor in integrated systems and project management with a traditional and agile approach. I am certified as PMI PMP and IDB PM4R.

I am an honest, cheerful, enthusiastic and creative person with an excellent ability and willingness to communicate ideas and inspire others. Passionate about educational projects, volunteering and social causes, working with animals and nature.

Diane Dromgold
Australia

RNC Global Projects / CEO

Q1• Describe your journey as a project management professional.

When I started in projects there were no courses to go on, no professional bodies to join, no conferences to attend, no methods, and no distinction between projects, programs and portfolios. Projects were either small or large and either had child projects or not. There was only one agenda and that was to deliver the desired outcome. If the desired outcome wasn't delivered the project was a failure. If it did, it was a success. I loved and still love the energy that's created by a group of people working towards a goal and having the relative freedom to do something others haven't yet done (at least in this specific context).

Becoming a project professional for me was about the mindset and the work rather than any qualification or certification.

I don't think I became a project professional as much as I was one and simply learned the trade. Often traveling to talk with people who stood out in their ability to deliver and never getting sidetracked by the race to the bottom of the lowest common denominator qualifications.

Q2• Why did you choose to become a project management professional?

See my bio. I chose it as a child. It's not what I wanted to be but who I was. Who I am. My choice was to be the best I could be and deliver as much as possible for as many people as possible. I am not an accidental project manager. I'm a deliberate project deliverer.

Q3• Have you encountered any related obstacles in advancing your career?

No, I think I've been lucky. I've been led by people who cared more about the outcome than my gender. There have been times when I've despaired at the preference for males in 'hard roles' but I don't think I've ever missed out. I just worked harder and was more convincing. Reflecting on this as a result of the question, I'd say I didn't follow a path, I made my own and while that takes a deal of determination and grit, you don't meet as many people with reasons to bring you down.

I do get annoyed though when I see conferences with no or token female presenters. In fact these days I simply don't go. It's my personal stand. No females, no Diane.

Q4• Why is it important that more people work in the project management area?

Actually, I'm not sure it is. There are millions of people in project management at the moment and frankly the profession has a pretty poor reputation.

I think it's more important that people who want to deliver targeted outcomes are drawn back to the profession. Over the years, the go getters have mostly got up and gone. They've been replaced with people who truly believe that procedure trumps action. I've often said if I was looking at the profession now, I'd probably have done something else.

Whatever we do, and whoever works in the profession, we must distinguish between project administration and project delivery. That's the key for the profession and the organisations needing outcomes.

Q5• How can we encourage more people to pursue project management as a career?

Put in place a distinction between admin and delivery. We need admins, we surely do, but we have way too many and was too few people with the skills and attributes to navigate ambiguity, to make things clear for others and absorb the stress to allow people to perform at their best. We need deliverers and they are not attracted to administration.

Q6• What do you think are the top issues that project managers face today?

Let me count them;

- *The rhetoric from professional bodies about qualifications equaling skills – it sets us and organisations up for disappointment.*
- *The commitment of a lot of people to believing the project can be successful even if the desired outcome is not delivered. This puts us at odds with the world. The only benefit from good admin when there is a failure; it is forensically defensible. In other words the PM has their butt covered.*
- *PMO's staffed by uber administrators. These PMOs add little value but are a significant overhead on projects, and often the relationship between deliverer and PMOs is antagonistic.*

- *The perception that PM doesn't add value to an organisation. We did that by insisting admin's value enough.*
- *If you can actually deliver desired outcomes you can also be a CEO – we lose many of the potential best to the bigger table.*

Q7• Do you think there is a stereotype attached to project managers?

Yes and it's a bit like librarians used to be and HR is now. If you can get away without them do it.

Q8• Why is it important to celebrate international women's day?

That's a left field question. We need to see and hear from people who've been there and done that. Role models and people to look up to. Most of all I think it's important as a chance to enjoy each other, have a laugh, and then get back to it. A bit like a locker room rev up.

Q9• On international women' s day, what is the most important message you offer to project management professionals?

You can do it. If it's what you want. There are much easier ways to make a living but if you've got the drive and clarity of thought and the desire to truly serve that's a start. If you don't want or need the glory and get excited by helping other people succeed, you might make it. Don't chase the quals down the rabbit hole. Actually make stuff happen and have some fun along the way. And get to know yourself. If you need patting and positive feedback perhaps there are other careers.

I'm very happy with my career and extremely lucky that I saw and admired Alan Stretton when I was a child. Find your Alan. Be inspired and go for it.

Diane Dromgold

On Christmas Day 1974, a cyclone hit and devastated Darwin in Northern Australia.

As a child Diane, with her family, watched news reports and listened to the radio for updates. It was distressing to see the pain and bewilderment of those impacted.

But by Christmas evening a man stood up and took charge of the immediate response and planning and delivering the rebuild of Australia's northernmost city. That man was Alan Stretton. Diane became fascinated with him, with his cool head, his clear thinking, his determination to do what was right, and his ability to do his job without fear of favor from competing interests.In the next days, weeks, and months, Diane followed Alan and his achievements. She decided to do whatever it took to be able to do what Alan was doing. To take on big challenges and deliver results, her future as a project deliverer was set.

Projects/programs and their delivery have been her focus throughout her career. She counts numerous countries, companies, industries, and approaches as part of her story so far. Never stop learning is one of her mottos. Diane continues to take on and deliver the hard and the hopeless. She started RNC Global Projects in February 1999, and she and the company are well- known for correcting and delivering projects and programs.

Almost every day, Diane can be heard saying 'administration doesn't get results, it's necessary but not sufficient, and if you only focus on administration you've already failed at delivery'.

In addition to running RNC, Diane has written one book, has another on the way, contributed to many others and loves an audience who really want to get to the nub of what it takes to make projects and programs succeed.

Emma Ruth Arnaz Pemberton
United Kingdom

Wellingtone / Director of Consulting Services

Q1• Describe your journey as a project management professional.

Like many people I 'fell' into project management when I woke up to being an accidental project manager. At the time I was helping to set up a new branch of the business I worked for in Europe, and a colleague referred to me as the project manager. Following this epiphany, I did research on what the role of a project manager was, and soon became proficient thanks to some recognized certifications. Over time, I worked as a Programme Manager, Change Manager, and eventually found PMO through attending industry events and hearing about it. Since choosing PMO as my focus area, I have been lucky enough to work across boundaries, and supported the PMO profession through my work with various associations and charitable organizations. And some of my clients have even won industry recognized awards!

Q2• Why did you choose to become a project management professional?

I didn't choose project management; I guess the saying goes project management chose me! I did however, choose PMO as my long term career after working as a PPM professional for a time.

I chose PMO because it is one of the professions that allows me to be connected to departments and people across organizations. Also, because every PMO is different, my days are varied and interesting all the time!

Additionally, I believe that PMO is one of the few professions where it is possible to see the value we add clearly and in lots of cases, clearly. It is a very rewarding place to sit in an organization if you are passionate about making a difference.

Q3• Have you encountered any related obstacles in advancing your career?

Being able to learn about topics that interested me when I was employed and my employer directed my development. I found that frustrating when I had things that I believed would add value to my role; which is why I devised the Wellingtone PMO Academy, an event that allows people to choose their best fit training package.

Q4• Why is it important that more people work in the project management area?

Part of the Association for Project Management's vision is 'project management is a life skill for all'. This resounds today, more than ever in the world we live in. It is volatile, uncertain, complex and ambiguous; meaning that some structure is required for almost everything we do.

Q5• How can we encourage more people to pursue project management as a career?

We need to focus on the young people who are going to be leading the work economy of the future. The Project Management Institute holds some events to introduce children to project management principles and I think this is the way forward.

Q6• What do you think are the top issues that project managers face today?

Keeping up with the emerging trends. So many PPM professionals are 'stuck' because they do not have the opportunity to learn about the new ways of working that could help them greatly in their role. We need to make things more accessible.

Q7• Do you think there is a stereotype attached to project managers?

Analytical and a good manager.

Q8• Why is it important to celebrate international women's day?

The history of the industry has been known to be male-focused. Although times have changed, and we see that balance more in the PMO space, it is important to remember that some found it hard to evolve their professional profile. On the flip-side of that, I do controversially think that we now need to start moving forward from this point of view, acknowledge the progress, and focus on the future.

Q9• On international women' s day, what is the most important message you offer to project management professionals?

Never stop learning.

Emma Ruth Arnaz Pemberton

Emma-Ruth Arnaz-Pemberton; a Fellow of the Association for Project Management is a PMO, Project, Programme and Portfolio specialist with extensive experience in the change management industry and a particular focus on collaboration, PMO conception & strategy, method and capability development.

As the Director of Consulting Services for Wellingtone Project Management, Emma-Ruth is responsible for all services PMO and PPM consulting area and organizes Wellingtone's two flagship annual events; the FuturePMO conference and Project Management Day of Service.

Jane Farley
New Zealand

Real Outcomes Limited / Director and Principle Consultant

Q1• Describe your journey as a project management professional.

I had an opportunity to join IBM as a senior project manager, after gaining my credential. In my ten years at IBM, I had many opportunities to work as a project manager, program manager and Quality Assurance Manager, working with a wide variety of customers and across multiple industries. At the same time I became the Professional Development Manager for IBMNZ and a member of the Australasian IBM Certification Review Board (CRB) for project managers. The CRB members review and recommend candidates for IBM's own internal project management credentials. Auckland City Council then, headhunted me to be their Portfolio Manager for the CBD into the Future, strategy implementation for the next seven years.

Since then, I have had a range of work opportunities, including being a PMO Director in Saudi Arabia, undertaking strategy development, developing Canadian University's distance learning course on Risk Management and as an operational manager of organizational performance and improvement. I am currently working at the University of Auckland on pan-university strategy development and implementation of strategic initiatives.

Since becoming a PMP, I have also been a volunteer within the profession, primarily so that I could give back to others in the profession. I have had a wide variety of opportunities, including leadership of a transformation project that saw the global introduction of new community models by PMI, I served on the global PMI Board of Directors for six years and am currently serving on the PMI Educational Foundation Board, where I was chair in 2019.

Q2· Why did you choose to become a project management professional?

As an Information Consultant, my first projects were to develop and implement new services for the National Library of New Zealand. I had not had much formal project management training, although reading "Thriving on Chaos" by Tom Peters, resonated with me so much, I remember telling my manager that I wanted a career as a project manager.

I joined the PMI New Zealand chapter to be able to learn from and network with more experienced project managers. I then found out about the project management professional (PMP) and joined a study group, because at that point, gaining knowledge and being able to apply what I learned was more important to me than the credential itself. However, I soon realized that I had the right experience for the credential and successfully gained my PMP.

Q3· Have you encountered any related obstacles in advancing your career?

Being prepared to move between organizations to advance my career and embracing opportunities as they arise has helped to mitigate any obstacles that have arisen. Mostly the obstacles have arisen through misperceptions about what my strengths and capabilities were and the potential roles I could take on. This meant I was being pigeon-holed.

Another obstacle was the opportunity for advancement (e.g. portfolio management) was just not available in the current organization. My career has been a serendipitous journey, but it is one where I have adapted and reinvented myself as necessary along that path.

Q4• Why is it important that more people work in the project management area?

Organizations are increasingly under pressure to have more agility, innovate, adapt to change and achieve strategic growth, increasing numbers of project managers will be required to bridge the gap from strategy to implementation, as they help drive the change, facilitate improvements and deliver innovation. A couple of years ago, PMI predicted that 2.2 million new project-orientated roles will be created every year until 2027, even with Gartner's prediction last year that 80% of all project management support or PMO tasks by 2030, will be replaced the growing use of AI, machine learning and robotic process automation.

Q5• How can we encourage more people to pursue project management as a career?

Project management is a career for people who are seeking a career that is meaningful, feel worthwhile, has an impact, adds value, and enables them to make a difference. We are told that this is what excites and motivates the younger generation. It is a career in which a person who embraces change can constantly be learning on a daily basis, which means stimulation and being challenged.

The demand and future prospects for advancement in project management are considerable, especially coupled with the transferable skills developed, such as leadership, managing people, setting direction and communicating expectations for the team, and a focus on goals and financial outcomes enables movement across industries and even promotion to senior and executive roles.

Q6• What do you think are the top issues that project managers face today?

Key trends that project managers are facing are numerous and diverse. Some have been around for the past five years, while others are still coming to the fore.

Constantly evolving digital technology that impacts not only the business solutions and organizational transformation that are being implemented, but also the advanced project management tools and solutions. Uses of artificial intelligence (AI) and automation are expanding at a rapid pace, and there is an increasing focus measurement through Business Intelligence (BI) and data analytics, on both project benefits and operational improvements.

Along with the growing importance of human-centred design, there is a need for a broader knowledge and skills set; including PMTQ (a person's ability to adapt, manage and integrate technology based on the needs of the organization or the project at hand), AI and robotics, and Emotional Intelligence (EI) and Emotional Quotient (EQ).

In the project management methodology arena, there is at last a growing acknowledgment of the need for blended methodologies through fusion, hybridization or customization. Whereas, there are many (including myself) who have long held the belief that it is important to use the methods, tools and techniques or combination that are most appropriate for the project and delivery of the solution.

There is a shifting and growing gig economy which has resulted in more remote or distributed teams made up of fewer full-time team members that supported by a widespread mobile network of freelancers. This can change the nature of a project management and where resources are in short supply can make the project management more challenging.

In an increasing competitive landscape, risk management becomes more important to an organization, while the rate of change in many organizations is resulting in increased organization wide collaborative leadership at many levels and leads to an increasing focus on change management. This is where some organizations are setting up a specialist change management practice in support of project management and operational continuous improvements.

Closer connections between strategy and the projects that contribute to the execution and achievement of its aspiration are growing, as executives and senior leaders are realizing the importance of this connection. Identified barriers stem from a wide range of issues including insufficient communication or information, lack of organizational agility, the culture, poor alignment of finances and resources, lack of appropriate capabilities and governance.

Q7•   Do you think there is a stereotype attached to project managers?

Some people see project managers as detailed, focused on plans, command control, being rigid, inflexible, not wanting any change in the project, being rather 'blinkered' and in a need to follow a specific methodology. This may reflect that they have been working with an inexperienced person who needs structure to define the framework within which they should work.

Whereas, an experienced project manager will be more comfortable with a focus on managing relations, communication, while doing what it takes to ensure things are done, done well and on time, by applying the most appropriate tools, techniques or methods for the initiative and making adjustments to the plan as they address changes and issues. All of this, while maintaining an awareness of strategic alignment and how the initiative fits within the bigger picture.

Q8•   Why is it important to celebrate international women's day?

In the project management profession, about 30% of project managers are female, and only 1% of females are likely to become a project director or board members compared with 4% of males, and reportedly there is 23.1% pay gap between males and females.

Celebrating the women that have a successful career and telling their stories can provide the inspiration as role models to the next generation, as well as motivating others to take the first or next step along their own path.

With the 2020 theme of "an equal world is an enabled world", it is important to recognize those female trail blazers that have gone ahead to shine the light on the possibilities and potentially made the path easier to follow.

Q9• On international women' s day, what is the most important message you offer to project management professionals?

Although some say the biggest obstacle is that many women will not or do not want to put in overtime, I have found this is equally balanced between males and females; it is choice based on their individual circumstances. If a woman wants to embrace change and has a strategic mindset, then she can help bridge the gap between strategy and driving implementation of the outcomes.

As females more likely to be transformational leaders, who serve as a role model, coach and mentor others develop their skills, are creative and motivated and dedicated to achieving the end goal, they are ideal attributes that will enable a successful career in project management.

Jane Farley

Ms. Farley is a proven leader whose career spans more than 30 years developing strategy and leading business performance/operations and has managed multi-million dollar projects, programs, and portfolios, in Australia, New Zealand, Canada and Saudi Arabia. She has a diverse background covering central, regional and local government, as well as a wide range of industries: information services, information technology, education, financial services, health, transportation, utilities and telecommunication.

As the owner and principle of Real Outcomes Limited, a NZ based consultancy, she focuses on strategy development and implementation. She is currently a Strategic Programme Manager with the University of Auckland based in the award-winning University Strategic Programme Office.

Ms. Farley is a former director on the YWCA Lower Hutt Board, served with LIANZ and the Australasian IT-19 Standards Committee. She has been a PMI volunteer since 1996, initially five years with PMI New Zealand, including the president, culminating in being awarded "Fellow of PMI New Zealand".

Over the past 16 years, she has served on several Member Advisory Groups and was a leader on the Community Transformation Project. She served six years on the global PMI Board Directors, where she held roles of Secretary/Treasurer, Chair Performance Oversight Committee, and Chair Strategic Development Oversight Committee. She is currently serving on the PMIEF Board of Directors (2017-2021), led several task teams, including strategy and is a past PMIEF Chair.

Ms. Farley's professional recognitions include IBM's global "2005 PM Excellence Award" for her program management expertise. She is a chartered member of the Institute of Directors (CMInstD) and a certified Management Consultant (CMC).

Ms. Farley holds a Master of Science (Zoology) and postgraduate Diploma of Librarianship from Victoria University of Wellington (Wellington, New Zealand). She obtained her PMP® designation in 1998, and graduated from the PMI Leadership Institute Masters Class in 2005.

Jennifer Young Baker

USA

University of Southern California / Associate Professor

Q1• Describe your journey as a project management professional.

My journey as a project professional began as an unintended one. I managed projects as part of my "regular job" and had not considered it as a career. By the time I was in my twenties, I had managed several projects. I started working at a regional bank as a contingent worker and then was hired full time employee, the majority of my work was managing projects. I did quite well at it and when the opportunity arose to manage projects as my full time job, I happily accepted. The professional journey has been a long but fruitful one. I have had the opportunity to become a credentialed professional many times over, travel the world and give back to others all along the way.

Q2• Why did you choose to become a project management professional?

I actually didn't choose the profession – it chose me.

Q3• Have you encountered any related obstacles in advancing your career?

Yes. When I was working at the bank, I had done quite well in my work in a relatively short time. So well, that I was being asked to train others as they joined the department and many of the sponsors for the more difficult projects were requesting me as the project manager. Yet, I was passed over for a promotion more than once. Finally, I asked my manager why. He told me that I was not credentialed, and I was a woman - I'd be leaving soon. It made me angry and more determined than ever - so I made it a goal from that point forward to get a new credential every 12-18 months. By doing this, it removed the only obstacle I could do something about... When the next time came around for promotions and raises, there was not valid, legal reason to pass me over again. Not only did I get that promotion - but I was given a bonus and raise to go along with the new title. Since then, I have earned seven certifications, an advanced degree and acquired executive training to ensure that lack of education or credentials is never a reason to be denied an opportunity to move ahead.

Q4• Why is it important that more people work in the project management area?

When you focus on one thing, you become an expert. You wouldn't ask Henry Ford to be an abstract artist, Usain Bolt to stand still or Dame Judy Dench not to perform. These individuals became the best in their respective fields by doing it over and over again – perfecting their craft. Managing projects is no different. The world is moving faster and faster. The number of inventions from the year 2000 until now, dwarfs the number from all time until that point. Nearly all of those inventions were created and brought to the marketplace through a project. With that great number, there is a huge need for project managers to help deliver those ideas into products and services for the marketplace.

Q5• How can we encourage more people to pursue project management as a career?

Like all things, we need to reinforce the value of what we do and not get lost in the minutia. We know a car will be delivered through an assembly line but the design work needs to happen first – that project is embedded in the engineering discipline because they understand the need. Architecture is no different. Neither is aerospace. That manner of understanding has become ingrained in those professions which has sustained the passage of time. Individuals should be shown that a project manager is more than someone who tells people what to do; it is someone who makes things happen... That's how humans went into space, drove a car and even communicate with one another.

Q6• What do you think are the top issues that project managers face today?

One thing I see daily, is people insisting on differentiation between waterfall and agile delivery to the point that good project managers are being denied work and projects are still suffering. Our project success rate is not improving as a general rule, yet we have more and more experience working in a project setting. We are focusing on the wrong things. For example, requirements are requirements whether they are in a backlog or a business requirements document (BRD). This is just formatting. The skills needed to elicit those requirements remain the same regardless of the document template or software package where they are housed.

Another thing I see regularly is misconception. There are two camps of this unfortunate circumstance. Those who think that passing a test makes them an expert (becoming certified) and those who think they don't need to pass a test to do this work (practitioners by doing). Everyone needs some knowledge to attempt a task and passing a test shows that you have the knowledge to complete the task. It doesn't say how well you will deliver and there is no replacement for experience. Managers need to assess individuals on their strengths and weaknesses. In most cases, the ideal candidate will have a combination of both education and experience.

Q7• Do you think there is a stereotype attached to project managers?

In some industries, I have found that this is still true; while in technology centered industries, there seems to be less convention associated with who project managers are and what they do, there are others like engineering and construction where this is still the case. Part of this may be due to a few factors – the maturity of project management in the industry, male domination in the role, and nature of the work.

Q8• Why is it important to celebrate international women's day?

Despite all the victories and hard work by many for hundreds of years, there are still a great many industries and professions that are dominated by men in all communities across the globe. Women overwhelmingly bear the brunt of poverty while they raise their children and the children of others. Women are still marginalized, discriminated against and suffer from abuse around the globe. Even in industrialized countries, women generally earn less money than a man performing that same job and some surveys show, upwards of half of the women in the workforce have experienced discrimination on the job. While in most industrialized countries, women have reached a milestone of 100 years of women's suffrage – some have just been given the ability to vote in the last twenty years. If you didn't know - it is still illegal in some places for women to have credit in their own name, drive a car or even leave their home without a male escort. Despite the globalization of our economies and the international nature of many of our projects, this type of injustice still occurs daily.

Q9• On international women' s day, what is the most important message you offer to project management professionals?

If you are a woman in the project management profession: Seek out other women for support and guidance. Don't give up – keep trying. This determination will not only help you reach your goal but it will make you an even better project manager.

If you are a man in the project management profession: Help women move forward and speak up when you see improper behavior. By not speaking up, you stand with the antagonist. When we work in a more diverse environment, we all improve from its strength and prosperity.

Jennifer Young Baker

Jennifer is a PfMP, PgMP, PMP, MBB, BRMP, SAFe-SA and ITIL certified manager with more than 30 years of experience in many business sectors including finance, government, hospitality, education, transportation, construction and energy. Her undergraduate work was completed at the University of North Carolina at Wilmington. She holds a master's degree from Northeastern University and is a graduate of the 2015 PMI Leadership Institute's Masters Class. She is currently a Portfolio Management Consultant at TIAA and an Assistant Professor at the University of Southern California. She is also very active with several non-profit organizations including serving on the Board of Directors as past president for the PMI-Metrolina chapter. Her chapter won the 2015 PMI Chapter of the Year award during her tenure as president. She is currently the PMI Region Mentor for the mid-Atlantic area of the United States.

In 2013, she was featured in a portfolio management article called "Going the Distance" in PM Network magazine. She was both an Alpha and Beta Contributor for PMI's "Navigating Complexity" guide published in 2014. She wrote a chapter in the Portfolio Management compilation edited by Dr. Ginger Levin entitled, "Portfolio Management: A Strategic Approach" which was released in October 2014. In November of 2015, www.projectmanagement.com published her article entitled, "The Power of Project Portfolio Management". She led a pilot study for PMI's Business Analysis framework leading project teams within Duke Energy. She has been a contributor for ITPMI for several years as well as developed master's degree programs at Wake Forest University, Georgetown University and the University of Southern California.

Lavetta T Stevenson

USA

Boeing / Sr. Project Specialist & Agile Transformation Lead

Q1· Describe your journey as a project management professional.

My journey as a project management professional came about as an evolution of various positions at Southwestern Bell Telephone Company (now knows as AT&T). Landing a full-time job as a software developer came about relatively easy looking back on the situation. At the time, I was so nervous that I too would be a graduate without a job; that was not the goal.

After several years as a computer programmer, I applied and accepted into the local area networking (LAN) group at Southwestern Bell. The entry of LANs was an exciting time in technology that moved the organization beyond sharing printers in workgroups but sharing resources throughout the building of approximately 5,000 employees. My responsibility included ensuring departments, ranging from 50 to 100 people, was able to use the new networked computer and printer accessible from the LAN.

The LAN group also had a helpdesk component that supported all the organizations. When I wasn't installing computers and printers on the network, I spent time on the helpdesk. As the team expanded, I became the Supervisor for approximately 20 employees and contractors. Quickly, I realized I didn't enjoy people reporting directly to me; I was dealing with who was in the office, taking sick leave, and at least one who didn't want to show up for work at all. He gave me no choice but to terminate his employment since he didn't enjoy coming to work and doing his job. At some point, the helpdesk grew out of the small closet-sized room and needed a new home. Moving the helpdesk is when I received my first project; moved the helpdesk from 16 to 21 floors. My job was to work with all the external groups, such as network – cabling/connectivity, facilities – furniture, facilities – space build-out, procurement – new hardware, to name a few.

By this time, my employment with Southwestern Bell extended for over ten years, and it was the best time I ever had at work. The Helpdesk move project was an assignment that ended after the successful move.

Mark Grisley referred me to an IT recruiter, who offered a deal that I could not refuse. Enterprise Rent-A-Car titled Project Manager was my first position.

It was exciting to work with a new group of people for 3 to 18 months and deliver on a goal that tied back to the strategy of executive management. The position allowed me to lead, solve problems, and communicate with others. Each project was focused on implementing new technology, for example, moving from a dial-up email to Microsoft Exchange for over 2,000 employees.

Q2•   Why did you choose to become a project management professional?

The challenge of creating something new and integrating it into the existing environment was appealing to me. Also, most of the projects that I worked on had an executive sponsor, which paved the way to get to know the executives.

Project Management was becoming a bonafide profession in that there was a rigorous certification process that solidified one completed education, real-work experience, and passed the test to become a PMI- Project Management Professional (PMI-PMP). The PMP exam was like the bar exam for lawyers or board-certified exam for doctors.

Q3• Have you encountered any related obstacles in advancing your career?

There were many obstacles in advancing my career; one, in particular, is the company I worked for at the time, did not offer any project management training. I stumbled upon the Project Management Institute one day and have never left the organization. It was PMI that coached and mentored me into the Project Manager that I become. Continuous improvement is constant, and PMI provided the local connections of like-minded people through its monthly dinner meetings. Within several years, I was one of the best project managers at my employer. I began to have a project sponsor request me to run their projects.

Q4• Why is it important that more people work in the project management area?

Great question. I searched the PMI site for some supporting data and found none.

The field of project management has begun to change from a strictly traditional only approach to a hybrid agile approach. With that said, there will be some existing traditional project managers not able to make the switch from traditional to agile as needed. Therefore, it will be necessary that more people work in the field of project management.

Q5• How can we encourage more people to pursue project management as a career?

There are many ways; however, the idea that sticks out most in my mind is allowing your actions to speak for itself. By this, I mean, love and express your passion about the profession, and people will notice.

As new interns groom for full-time employment at my present employer, as a project manager/scrum master/scrum coach, I get so excited about the work that I do; several interns have chosen the field of project management.

Q6• What do you think are the top issues that project managers face today?

There is one particular issue facing project managers that I am passionate about, and it is called Agile Transformation. Agile allows the team to learn early in the process and stay connected to the customer throughout the process. As a traditional project manager, I strongly encourage you to learn as much about project delivery or product delivery using agile. With the advent of the Agile Manifesto in 2001, a better way of developing software exist. Agile done correctly has proven time and time again to be a benefit to the team, customer, and organization.

Q7• Do you think there is a stereotype attached to project managers?

I am unaware of a stereotype attached to project managers. An effective project manager influences the servant leadership style. Command and control project managers are not the most sought after in the world of Agile.

Q8•   Why is it important to celebrate international women's day?

International Women's Day is very critical to uplift all women in all countries, no matter what race or color. It is one day, but we as women should always champion each other in the name of sisterhood, especially those who have achieved social, economic, and political achievements. Mark your calendar for March 8, 2020.

Q9•   On international women's day, what is the most important message you offer to project management professionals?

One of the essential messages to project management professionals is to stay passionate about our profession, reach back, and bring someone forward. Stretch yourself to engage in a group of like-minded people via meetup, local event or international event.

Lavetta Thomas Stevenson

Lavetta Thomas Stevenson is Sr. Project Special/Agile Transformation Coach for Boeing in the Information Technology (IT) organization in Missouri. As a servant leader, Lavetta splits her time between Digital Common Services and Enterprise IT Operations within IT. In each department, she leads one or more teams to deliver business value.

Previously, Lavetta was a project management consultant in the finance, car rental, pharmacy benefits management, and telecommunication industry. She has managed projects with 10 to 25 people; $500K to $2.1 mil. An example of projects Lavetta managed:

(1) Pattern Day Trader - provided new compliance software that provided the checks and balances needed to monitor investment day traders

(2) LAN Inc Helpdesk move - moved a helpdesk to a larger space

(3)Network From Everywhere - delivered a new WAN and LAN along with a new Infoblox implementation.

Lavetta has spent her spare time with her husband of 31 years and two adult children. Over the years she has volunteered to give back to the community as Secretary for Mentor St. Louis, Director of Certifications for PMI - St. Louis Chapter, Board member of Southern Illinois University – Edwardsville Alumni, and panel member for the United Way of Greater St. Louis Funding Panel.

Lori Nevin
USA

Triumph Integrated Systems / Senior Program Manager

Q1• Describe your journey as a project management professional.

I was managing projects for my own consulting/contracting business for 13 years without formal project management training. During that time out of need, I learned through trial and error and implemented the processes that I later formally studied. I was doing the right thing and didn't know it.

Q2• Why did you choose to become a project management professional?

After I decided to re-join the corporate world, I was employed as a Marketing Assistant at a company that had very formal project management processes for software implementations. The company asked me to take on project coordination under an experience project manager. Through that colleague that had her PMP certification, and from those experiences, I learned I and thoroughly enjoyed project management. I decided to continue down that professional path.

Q3• Have you encountered any related obstacles in advancing your career?

One obstacle is that I do not have a technical degree or background. During the recession, companies asked their technical people to manage projects because the companies had to do more with less. I was unemployed for over a year, and then under-employed for another year.

Another obstacle is that I did not have an undergraduate degree until this year. When applying for project management jobs, I was unsuccessful competing with PMPs who also had a Bachelor's degree.

Q4• Why is it important that more people work in the project management area?

I believe that companies that projectize their work and have an experienced project manager leading their strategic efforts are more successful completing projects.

Q5• How can we encourage more people to pursue project management as a career?

Job shadowing a project manager was what encouraged me to pursue this career. I think mentoring or having someone shadow my work gives others a very good example of the work we do. Then an individual can have a real-life understanding of what it takes to be a PM. I would like to see that we implement some video stories of PMs that can go out to primary and secondary schools. The videos would show real people that have become successful project managers, that tell their stories. Especially a story like mine, given I was self-made.

Q6• What do you think are the top issues that project managers face today?

The top issues today are the watering down of the PMP certification, and the need to practice the basic fundamentals of project management, especially the planning processes. Often our company leaders don't want to give us the time to do the fundamentals of our job.

Q7• Do you think there is a stereotype attached to project managers?

Definitely. When I start at a new company, I can see that I have to set about changing the mindset that others see project managers as nagging people that just get in their way of doing their work.

Q8• Why is it important to celebrate international women's day?

In the aerospace industry that I'm in, I can expect to be the only woman in our internal team, and the only woman interacting with the customer teams. It's rare that I interact with other women, unless they are in more traditional women's roles such as accounting, human resources, or administration. Celebrating International Women's Day should spotlight women in less traditional roles.

Q9• On international women' s day, what is the most important message you offer to project management professionals?

Yes, there are women CEOs and CFOs. Yes, there are women in accounting, human resources, or administration. AND here we are, in the middle! Showcase women project managers, quality engineers, manufacturing technicians and others.

Lori Nevin

Lori Nevin, Certified Project Management Professional (PMP) since 2009, has practiced Project Management, Marketing and Customer Service Management in the non-profit sector, automotive, aerospace, manufacturing industries, and managed programs for software and hardware integration as well as hardware new product design, development, production and market introduction. Organizations have trusted Lori with their most strategic customers to solve problems, to achieve program objectives, and to move the organization from the present into the future.

Lori's work has been held up to satisfy internal, customer, and independent project management process audits. Where there are no processes in place, Lori will document systems and repeatable processes to make work more efficient. Lori provides a structured approach to ongoing professional development and creating community for herself, her colleagues and her teams. Her approach integrates smoothly with staff initiatives. Lori credits the many professional, educational, industry networks and resources that she has available.

Lori has been awarded 4-H Youth Development Program Leader of the Year, PMI Chapter Volunteer of the Year, and Zodiac Aerospace Site Team Member of the Month. Lori has been a speaker at the Pacific NW Aerospace Alliance Women in Aerospace Conference, Women of Washington State in Aerospace, and the Mount Baker Chapter PMI. Lori's creative writing has been expressed in travel blogs, children's books, poems, and editorial, with published works in print media, and in e-news publications.

LuAnn Piccard

USA

University of Alaska Anchorage / Project Management Department Chair
and Associate Professor

Q1•   Describe your journey as a project management professional.

I earned my engineering degree in engineering/product design in the mechanical engineering department at Stanford University. My first job right out of college was with Hewlett Packard as a development engineer. I was designing fiber optics transmitters and receivers. At that time, I didn't even understand what project management was. I was part of a development team and working on that project, I got an idea of what it was like to work with different people in teams developing products and completing projects.

That's really where my journey started. I found that I wasn't necessarily cut out to be the "genius engineer", the person who is the super technical expert. But what I was good at defining what we needed to do and then often finding the thing that people hadn't found before—the idea or the solution—that hadn't been considered, and then mobilizing people to get that done. And so, from that very first project I found that as a project manager, my skills were different than the traditional skills of the engineers I worked with. I was often the only

100

woman on the team, and I think I brought different skills from that perspective, as well.

I became acquainted with Project Management Institute when I was leading one of the larger organizations at HP. It had a professional services component in which our consultants were going around the world and helping customers deploy telecommunication networks. My team came to me and said, "There's this thing called a PMP where we have the opportunity to get credentialed. It will help us when we say we're from California, but we're helping someone in Singapore. We will have the credibility, they will understand that we're professionals as project managers".

I had several people in my organization get credentialed as PMPs, and that was when I really became acquainted with project management as a profession—a standalone profession—as opposed to something that happened inside of an organization. As an individual, I started having an affinity for it, then doing it in every stage of my career at varying levels, and then ultimately leading organizations where that was the main emphasis of what people in the organization did on behalf of the customers.

Q2• Why did you choose to become a project management professional?

Interestingly enough, I didn't get my PMP until I left the tech sector and came back into academia. I felt like I had been a PMP my whole career, but I just never received the credential.

I'm originally from Alaska and when my daughter was born, I was traveling sixty percent of the time. I didn't want to miss out on being a mom. My husband and I then decided to retire out of tech, and we came back to Alaska to raise our daughter closer to family. That's when we both joined the University of Alaska Anchorage as professors.

I was part of the project management department, and since we were affiliated with PMI and going through the accreditation process with GAC, I decided to get my PMP. I chose to get my PMP, because I felt like it gave me credibility with the students I was teaching.

Q3• Have you encountered any related obstacles in advancing your career?

I don't really see obstacles—I always see challenges. Every job that I have ever had, was one that people didn't think could be done, didn't want to do or felt was impossible. I gravitate to those positions because I see them as interesting challenges, and I believe that anything can be overcome. So, I see things less as obstacles, and more as opportunities to prove that something is possible.

The challenges I've had were exciting to me because I was looking into the white space; working with customers to figure out what they wanted to accomplish and find out what is driving their need set. In each situation, it's a challenge to figure out how to do that, but when you find a solution, you feel like you've hit something on all cylinders.

As an example, in college I was working as a biomedical engineer at the Rehab Engineering R&D Center in Palo Alto. I was working with people who had recently been injured, and my boss came to me and said, "Design something that will help in their rehabilitation".

Rehabilitation can mean a lot of things. It's not just your physical rehabilitation; these young men had accidents in the prime of their life, and now, suddenly, their life was going to be quite different because of the injuries they had suffered. They needed to think about their mental health, their social, spiritual and physical heath because all those things together are what really help somebody to overcome a challenge, or obstacle in life.

One day it came to me—the idea of designing a shoulder-operated controller for a Space Invaders video game. When attached to someone's shoulder using a harness, it was controlled like a joystick positioned on its side. The character moved left to right on the screen when the user moved their shoulder forwards and backwards. A missile was fired when they moved their shoulder up and down. A therapist could calibrate the device so that it could require more or less, motion as the person increased their capability. It would challenge them, but it was also something fun. And I designed it so that two people could play it at the same time and compete.

In doing this, I found that I was able to observe other people overcoming challenges through the work I was doing, and it was gratifying. I could see in their eyes that they then understood that with just a little bit of adaptation, they could be equal to or better than someone who didn't have that same limitation. To me, I always think of obstacles as challenges and opportunities because than give you an opportunity to innovate and be different and do things differently. Inspired by this experience and the difference I could make, I realized my mission was to design solutions that changed peoples' lives.

Q4•   Why is it important that more people work in the project management area?

The world, innovation and opportunity are all fueled by projects. Projects empower people to make ideas a reality and produce positive outcomes that make a difference in the world.

If we want to make the world a better place, if we want to create value and opportunities for our customers and for people in our communities, then it's all going to be done through projects. And the better we are at doing that, the quicker we add value and the more value we add.

Q5• How can we encourage more people to pursue project management as a career?

I love what our PMI Education Foundation is doing with bringing project management skills to our youth, particularly the five to nineteen age group. That's where people start to realize their capability to get things done through project work. They may not initially realize they have the capacity and the opportunity to turn what they are good at into a career. I think in some cases, they see it as a way to get something done, rather than a career that they may pursue.

As an educator, I get the chance to do workshops at my university for kids in K-12 who are considering careers in engineering, technology and project management. It's an opportunity to help these kids understand what project management is about. It's a life skill, not just a profession.

By teaching kids about project management early on in their educational careers, we can help them become better students. They get their work done in a more efficient way, and they produce better outcomes. The better they are at that, the more successful they are as students. Then they may realize that doing this at a professional level is something that they are particularly good at.

I would say one of the things that I am constantly impressed by is the number of women who are awesome at project management. I think we sometimes have a natural affinity towards complicated things, holistic thinking, multitasking, and lots of things going on at one time. And to be a good project manager, you must be able to keep all things moving and understand the influence of one thing on another. I find that a lot of young women discover how incredibly good they are at this, and they become exceptional project managers as a result. The earlier we can help people understand what project management is and the value it can bring to their life and professional opportunities it opens, the more people we will see coming into the profession.

Q6• What do you think are the top issues that project managers face today?

I think perhaps its people understanding that project management is a profession and the value of it; as a profession. A lot of people do project work, but they may not do it necessarily in a way that's going to deliver outcomes as effectively as they could. Because there is so much work that gets done as a project, many people are project managers or project personnel, but they may not necessarily have the skill set they need to be as effective as possible.

A really interesting opportunity I find exciting with project management is; all the changes in technology, artificial intelligence, machine learning and all these new emerging ways of working and how organizations are transforming themselves to be able to do more interesting things, better and faster. This presents a huge opportunity for our project managers to go in and help organizations determine how to complete projects effectively. A lot of people are afraid of what these changes may bring, but I think project managers can demonstrate that by utilizing those tools effectively; even greater value can be added and faster.

Rather than an obstacle or a challenge in a negative sense, I think a challenge in a positive sense as how our project managers can go in, utilize those capabilities and really impact in a positive way, the outcomes that organizations are looking to produce.

Q7•   Do you think there is a stereotype attached to project managers?

I think there can be a stereotype that project management is a heavy, methodical "follow the rules" kind of approach, rather than a flexible framework that incorporates a range of methodologies adapted to meet specific needs. Many situations require and benefit from a more methodical, well-planned approach and others need to be highly iterative given uncertainty and the need for speed. Regardless of the methodology chosen, projects and project managers produce change and everything about a project is doing something different and innovating the way you produce outcomes as much as what the outcomes are.

Project management is found everywhere. It's being agile, being nimble, tailoring practices of project management inside of organizations to fit for purpose for what the work needs to be done and how it needs to be done to produce the outcomes that you're looking for. Project management is being flexible, adaptable and being able to work with all different kinds of people to get things done effectively.

Q8•   Why is it important to celebrate international women's day?

Women represent at least half of our world's population and are doing incredible things. Women often face unique challenges to be able to demonstrate the value they bring to organizations and communities.

As a woman myself, I've come up through a career path that was traditionally male dominated, and I found that the skill sets women have been different. And celebrating difference is important. I think women bring different perspectives and points of view, when we combine those, with all different kinds of people, we can accomplish more by celebrating and benefiting from our differences.

Celebrating International Women's Day is simply a way of acknowledging that people with different perspectives have a voice and have an opportunity to bring these perspectives to the table and change, improve and shape outcomes that are going to be even more exceptional for organizations and our communities.

Q9·   On international women' s day, what is the most important message you offer to project management professionals?
Simply, use your difference to make a difference. Bring those perspectives that are uniquely yours and make your voice heard. Help shape the conversation in ways that improve outcomes and create lasting differences.

LuAnn Piccard
LuAnn Piccard, PMP, associate professor and chair of the Project Management Department at the University of Alaska Anchorage, is passionate about developing next-generation project management leaders/ professionals seeking to enhance and expand career opportunities through professional development and higher education. Students and graduates have benefited from the depth, relevance and

breadth of Piccard's seasoned executive experience, transforming the learning environment into a rigorous, positive, collaborative and applied experience.

Piccard brings over 20 years of experience in technology-sector project and portfolio management, including ten years as a senior executive for Hewlett Packard, Agilent Technologies, and Advanced Energy Industries, where she led complex, profitable, and cross-functional businesses serving customers worldwide. Piccard credits professional success of collaboration with diverse, engaged, customer-centric program and project leaders globally.

Piccard, proud PMI and PMI Alaska Chapter member, volunteer, and PMP since 2007, served as director and chair for the PMI Global Accreditation Center for Project Management Education Programs, responsible for project management academic program accreditation and quality assurance worldwide.

Inspired by community engagement, Piccard is well-versed in the balanced strategic and fiduciary responsibilities of board governance partnered with executive and operational leadership. She has served as volunteer director for 11 different non-profit boards including ten years as an officer and director for Habitat for Humanity of Anchorage.

Malgorzata Kusyk
Poland

AgilePMO / Founder

Q1•   Describe your journey as a project management professional.

I have a MSc degree in oceanography. (I am a marine biologist by background.) As a university student I decided to go to London to discover the world and learn more useful stuff. Finally, I learned English, discovered myself and opened to diversity; the skills I currently.

After three years I came back to Poland, and started working for Ericsson, the first mobile network in Poland in late 90s. There, when I found my first project, fell in love with project management. Since then project management has become my passion. Five years later, I moved to a production company joining the R&D department where I was responsible for electronic equipment design and production implementation projects and setting up a Project Management Office (PMO). I was also assigned to manage and successfully completed an organizational change program; including the company strategy, the organizational structure and culture, key processes mapping, balance scorecard and talent management areas. Again after 5 years joined Reuters (Thomson Reuters now) as a project manager responsible for a transition program (including the property and technology fit-out, recruitment and transition of 800 staff to Poland), which we successfully completed. As well as, consolidation and integration of Thomson and Reuters, migration of infrastructure, software upgrades or the implementation of Scrum and Agile philosophy. I have also defined and implemented some project management training programs awarded platinum "Above and Beyond Award".

In 2013, I founded my own company AgilePMO where we design and deliver innovative project management and leadership programs. We also support clients in transformation and transition projects, including agile transformations.

Meantime I had competed a project management post graduate studies and obtained some certifications – PMP®, PRINCE2®, AgilePM®, SMP® and Master Business Trainer. For 12 years I have been volunteering for Project Management Institute® taking different roles such as a branch director, a conference content reviewer, PMI® Educational Foundation Liaison and PMI Poland Chapter President 2014-2016. My work has been appreciated and awarded the Volunteer of the Year 2015 – The Best Leader title.

Q2• Why did you choose to become a project management professional?

As I mentioned before, that was an accident as the first project was not assigned to me, but I found it. I always stress that project managers need to be proactive – instead of waiting should act! There was a problem and I volunteered to help. Good relationships with both the client and the teammates helped us to find and deliver a solution in one location. Due to this success, I was formally assigned to manage the project in the second location where we experienced the same challenge, but there was no one to take the ownership of resolving the problem. That was the time I realized I was born for project management and started pursuing my career in that field in more structured and planned way. Then I took an in-house three-day course called PROPS for Project Managers delivered by Ericsson's Project Management Institute and using project risk management words was an exploited opportunity.

Q3• Have you encountered any related obstacles in advancing your career?

For a woman with no engineering background, it might be challenging to get a project management position in technology, including IT or construction which present much more project management opportunities. Although not every recruitment was successful, I was brave and diligent enough to try, again and again, until I found a company with open-minded managers who believed that project management is about people and the project manager's role is in 90% communication as PMBOK® Guide states.

Q4• Why is it important that more people work in the project management area?

No matter what industry you are in, there will be increasing project management opportunities. Organizations live in permanent change and that means that more jobs for project management related roles will be needed:

The Anderson Economic Group (AEG) analysis finds the project management profession will outperform total U.S. job growth over the next decade, creating millions of new positions that pay highly-competitive wages. Project Management Job Growth and Talent Gap 2017–2027 reveals that through 2027, the project management labor force is expected to grow by 33 percent. That means 22 million new jobs will be created during the next 10 years and by 2027 organisations will need nearly 88 million individuals working in project management-oriented roles.

Q5•   How can we encourage more people to pursue project management as a career?

Promote project management as skills for life and start teaching at school. I really like to quote Tom Taylor, Vice President of Association for Project Management: "Most of us manage projects, full-time, part-time and sometimes".

As a part of my PMI® Educational Foundation Liaison role I was responsible for introducing project management to schools. We were very successful to run project management workshops for youth and educators. At the moment we are working on a new initiative based on Scrum and eduScrum called, gameScrum; is about teaching and learning school subjects through playing and delivering projects using the Scrum framework. School doesn't have to be boring. We want to show that mathematics, physics, chemistry or biology can be learned while playing together, alongside gaining the competences of the future such as creativity, critical thinking, teamwork, or empathy.

Q6•   What do you think is the top issues today facing project managers in roles like yours?

Generally speaking, we all facing a VUCA (Volatile /Uncertain/Complex/ Ambiguous) world. That means fast and unpredictable change has become the norm and therefore, project manager's role needs to change. The new employer-desired skill set captured in the Project Management Institute (PMI) Talent Triangle® is a combination of project management technical, leadership, strategic

112

and business management expertise. Companies need project practitioners with leadership and business intelligence skills to support long-range strategic objectives. According to PMI's Pulse of the Profession® report, when organizations focus on all three skill sets, 40 percent more of their projects meet goals and original business intent. Today's project manager should be a leader of change and transformation. However, most of the current project management programmes on the market focus mainly on methods, tools and techniques (one side of the triangle). They rarely teach managers how to lead people through change. You can hardly find any learning modules on leadership, including dealing with uncertainties and ambiguities, conducting difficult conversations or managing the sociopolitical complexity in which transition projects are conducted.

As much as 39% of respondents of the survey conducted in New Zealand, (also similar to European conditions), highlighted that leading change in their organisation is a top gap, while 34% identified difficult conversations and conflict management as missing key competences. Another 30% of research participants mentioned the importance of political 'smarts' and resolving 'gray' issues. And 27% responded that communication is still a challenge. Here I would like to draw attention specifically to the techniques of active listening and non-violent communication (NVC) used in agile and teal organisations.

Q7• Do you think there is a stereotype attached to project managers?

Let me share a short story my friend who is a project manager overheard in a cafe. A couple talking:

> *A: I would like to be a project manager?*
> *B: Would you like to prepare PowerPoint presentations?*

113

For many people project management is just about preparing tons of documents and a project manager is a controlling nightmare.

Q8• Why is it important to celebrate international women's day?

To highlight that women are as much important as men and that together we can make a difference.

Q9• On international women' s day, what is the most important message you offer to project management professionals?

Be brave, discover yourself and live your values and support other women.

Malgorzata Kusyk

Project Manager and Agile Expert, AgilePMO Founder/CEO, Kozminski Executive Business School Coordinator, PMI Poland Chapter President 2014-2016. Mentor, business trainer, MBA lecturer and speaker worldwide. PMP®/PRINCE2P®/AgilePM®/PSM® certifications holder. Titled "Strong Women in IT 2019" by Come Creations Group Raport.

Małgorzata is a project management expert with 19 years of experience of managing global projects and programmes across multiple industries. She is an agility and team ambassador, specializing in transition and transformation initiatives, where she combines Agile with traditional approaches. She is the creator of some innovative business solutions and training programs - the founder of the first Transition Manager Academy and the co-founder of Akademia Zwinnej Liderki (Agile Women Leader Academy). Małgorzata is the author of many articles and an Agile HR chapter of HR Business Partner book. She is known for creativity and openness to experiments, so the solutions she proposes are unique and tailored to the needs of the client. Like Michael Jordan, Małgorzata believes that "Talent wins games, but teamwork and intelligence wins championships".

Margarida Goncalves (Dr.)
Portugal

Quasinfalível / CEO

Q1• Describe your journey as a project management professional.

I have been a project manager for the last thirty years. I studied applied maths and started my career as a programmer. Rapidly moved into team management and later to project management. In the 90´s there were a lot of big projects on Telco Companies and Banks, and I worked with local consultancy companies and the big 5 projects that transformed the way people work in Portugal. Teams were mixed and, even though we worked a lot, it was fun, and I have good memories of big and long projects, some up to five years. After 2000, I have started with more projects abroad and then I noticed that, landscape of project management in Africa was mainly a man´s land. It was difficult to have working conditions and difficult to be respected. In twenty years, a lot has changed for the better, but a lot needs to be done yet. This is why all our stories are important. I admit, I have felt more the bias towards women at management level, mostly when the corporate ladder is involved. Men tend to promote men; it is easier for them. As a result, I have my own consulting company on the last ten years and have actively contributed to the Portuguese and International Project Management Associations, respectively APOGEP (Associação

Portuguesa de Gestão de Projectos) and IPMA (International Project Management Association). I believe in the power of participation and that we all can create a better world.

Q2• Why did you choose to become a project management professional?

I am not sure if I chose to be a project management professional or if the profession chose me. I have always been a very organized and goal oriented person. I love to work with people and challenge them. In my first years as a project manager, I was more General than I am today. I discovered that life has its own flow and projects need to adapt to it instead of fighting it. While working with other professionals, I always found out that systematizing ideas was a fun thing, so I started to collaborate on standard writing and revision. That is a challenge, we have to reach consensus with people from all over the world and deliver consistent standards. I worked in IPMA ICB (Individual Competence Baseline for projects, programs and portfolios) and IPMA ICB CCT (Individual Competence Baseline for Consultants, Coaches and Trainers). Now, I am helping new countries to set-up their project management associations and it is a different kind of challenge. It is a more organizational challenge, than to be able to deliver on time and on budget. It is clearly a project where the quality of the outcome is more crucial than the timing. The set-up of project management associations throughout the globe is essential, to foster the professional, to get it recognized and to build foundations for better and more professionals. Project management is recognized in engineering, but on other areas, it is approached with much less rigor. A lot of project managers start as so, and then have to move to line management positions to be recognized in their companies.

Q3• Have you encountered any related obstacles in advancing your career?

I did, during my first years, and mostly on advancing my career on big corporations. I want to believe than nowadays things have changed for the better. I really do not know, because I have created my own company, and we have a different culture.

Q4• Why is it important that more people work in the project management area?

While having more people is important, it is crucial as well that better project managers are trained. In IT, my area, we have a lot of new methodologies for work management have been introduced, mostly around Agile. These methodologies were very good to focus people on smaller goals and to create pace and a culture of delivery that can absorb change and see it as part of the process. This has been a huge advance and different roles have emerged, such as Agile Coaches, Agile Leaders, etc. In some companies the project manager is seen as an old-fashioned term, but in the end, we are all delivering value to customers, independently of the role we are labeled.

Q5• How can we encourage more people to pursue project management as a career?

We need to recognize the profession in more countries, we need to have it as a mandatory discipline, not only in engineering schools but in all other schools, as well. In medical schools, it is normal to work as teams, but no project management techniques were taught. And, to be clear, project management techniques involve practice, people and perspective competences (please check ICB for competence elements on this subject).

Q6•   What do you think are the top issues that project managers face today?

Top issues today, as I perceive it, are all related with people management. Project managers tend to prefer tools to interact with people and do not recognize yet that communication has techniques and tools, as time management has. A lot has been achieved, and with the introduction of coaching on the area, a lot has improved, but there is still a long path to be walked through.

Q7•   Do you think there is a stereotype attached to project managers?

I really don't but if there is, I would say it is related more with the technical side of planning than with the negotiation and communication skills of project management. This is why it is still mainly a man´s world. The numbers are very clear in our associations.

Q8•   Why is it important to celebrate international women's day?

It is important to celebrate all the good things that happened in part of the globe, in order to give hope to those women living in countries, where the reality is different. Have them supported and make them believe in better and more equal opportunities.

Q9•   On international women' s day, what is the most important message you offer to project management professionals?

Women are as capable as men to be excellent project managers. The world is a better place when equal opportunities are in place.

Margarida Goncalves

Margarida Goncalves is a project manager and a consultant. She works with IT companies to recognize their excellence in project management by certifying them in CMMI and their individuals in IPMA 4LC. She is an Agile Coach and President of the Certification Board of APOGEP. She loves the profession, and she believes professionals need to keep pace in the VUCA world.

Merete Munch Lange
Norway

Miles Oslo AS / Senior Consultant/Project Leader

Q1• Describe your journey as a project management professional.

My journey started right after I finished university. I was hired as an information officer in a bank in Denmark, and an opportunity to lead a digital sales training program came up. I didn't hesitate to accept the offer – even though I didn't have any project management training. It was a steep learning curve, but I never regretted taking the leap.

Since then, I have managed projects in many different areas – from software development projects to organizational change projects. I started out being a project manager and I have evolved into a project leader, where leadership of people is my primary focus.

Q2• Why did you choose to become a project management professional?

As many of my colleagues, I became project manager by accident. I did not choose an education within the profession, my training and education on the job came later as well as courses and certifications. I have slowly moved into specializing in the organizational change area. It's all about people; help them to overcome fear and resistance to change seriously, and to help the organization to succeed. That could e.g. be helping to find new ways of working to realize benefits of implementing new IT systems.

Q3• Have you encountered any related obstacles in advancing your career?

Most of my work life has been in male dominated environments. There were times, when I felt that I had to work harder, just because of my gender, especially in the beginning of my career.

Q4• Why is it important that more people work in the project management area?

Organizations need project leaders who bring holistic perspectives, a deep curiosity and broad skill sets to the work at hand. That means an increased demand for versatile and bold project leaders—capable of embracing new ways of working, leading diverse teams and exploring innovative solutions.

Q5• How can we encourage more people to pursue project management as a career?

I think that leading by example and showing results, can inspire others to pursue a career within this area.

Q6• What do you think are the top issues that project managers face today?

In my opinion, the key is to choose the right way of working for every project. There is no 'one size fits all', and the future Project Manager must be more in touch with the unique needs and demands of the organization they work for. The number of stakeholders is increasing to a larger extent, and they represent more areas of the organization than previously, and we need to speak their language.

Q7• Do you think there is a stereotype attached to project managers?

I think we are moving away from the stereotypes. We have the project managers with an engineer background, and also we have the agile society where people have more diverse backgrounds as well as a different approach towards projects.

Q8• Why is it important to celebrate international women's day?

In 2020, one would take for granted that men and women are equal – in all aspects of life. We know that this is not the case! I see the International Women's Day as an opportunity to celebrate the women who have paved the way and gotten us to where we are today – at the same time, the day is a reminder of a job still to be done! It is important to continue to support our leaders, innovators, and risk-takers for thinking forward and expanding the possibilities for women around the globe.

Q9• On international women' s day, what is the most important message you offer to project management professionals?

Keep showing the world that professionalism has nothing to do with gender but everything to do with passion.

Merete Munch Lange

Merete Munch Lange has a major in Film, TV and Communications from the University of Copenhagen. She is Danish living in Norway and has worked in many global organisations. Merete has been a project leader for many years and has a certification in PRINCE2 foundation, she is a certified Scrum Master, and she is a PMP. Merete' s volunteer career in PMI started in 2008 and since then she has had many different roles. In PMI Norway Chapter she started as communication officer, before she moved on to become volunteer director and branch director. She went on to become the president of the chapter for four years, before she was appointed as Region Mentor for PMI Region 8 North West, a position she currently holds.

Merete is a senior consultant at Miles Oslo, a consultancy company which practices trust-based leadership and whose DNA is professionalism and warmth. Merete is a devoted servant leader with special interest in organizational development and cultural change.

She has been a speaker at numerous events, often on the topic of how to build trust teams.

Mona Fazel

Iran

PMO Global Alliance / Project Management Professional and PMO Global

Awards Judging Committee Member

Q1• Describe your journey as a project management professional.

When my career began in 2005, I was unfamiliar with project management, since I worked as a quality engineer in a manufacturing company. After almost a year in that role, I decided to leave the company, and next joined a project-oriented consulting firm as a Systems and Quality Engineer. In this role, I was a member of one of the company's support departments, where my job mostly involved establishment, implementation and maintenance of the corporate quality management system. During this period, I had the opportunity to work closer to project teams, and became increasingly attracted to the dynamic and challenging environment of project management. In 2009, as a result of my expressed interest in the field, I was able to join the project management team as a Project Planning and Control Engineer.

I was so excited about my new job as it suited my capabilities and strengths. Since I was so passionate about this field, I decided to pursue and successfully obtained my Project Management

125

Professional (PMP) certificate from the Project Management Institute in the United States in 2010. Soon after completing my PMP, I was promoted to Senior Project Planning and Control Engineer. Furthermore, in 2012, I was assigned as the Head of Project Management Office, as the first woman ever to be given such a role.

Q2• Why did you choose to become a project management professional?

The project environment has always been so dynamic and attractive to me. Bringing different personalities and capabilities together as a team to reach a unique goal is the challenge I enjoy. The other amazing fact about the projects is that despite having similarities with each other, each project is unique in various aspects, and as a result each new project challenges your technical, leadership and interpersonal skills in different ways. Having worked as the Head of a Project Management Office, I have had this amazing opportunity to be involved with several projects, facing their problems, addressing their challenges and experiencing their successes. This has made this field even more interesting to me.

Q3• Have you encountered any related obstacles in advancing your career?

Absolutely! Like many women working in male-dominated environments, I have faced several challenges to progress as a project management professional. Feeling underestimated due to your gender is what many women experience, especially during their early career. However, I believe that this could be considered as an opportunity for growth in long term, once women equip themselves with knowledge and build their confidence.

The other challenge has been working under high levels of uncertainty. This increased the level of projects dynamism and required quick decision-making and problem solving skills. Sometimes, even the most precise estimates were made irrelevant by drastically changed macroeconomic conditions.

Q4• Why is it important that more people work in the project management area?

Today the world is fast-paced and filled with many opportunities for growth. Governments are seeking to improve the quality of life in different countries. Several infrastructural, building construction, IT and industrial projects are planned annually to reach this goal. As a result, more skilled project management professionals are required.

Organizations need to have a clear framework and processes when it comes to managing projects. This will ensure successful results in managing project challenges by applying a systematic approach.

Q5• How can we encourage more people to pursue project management as a career?

It is important to emphasize to persons considering project management as a career, that as a project manager, each project will be a learning experience for you to grow and develop. Also, the challenge of dealing with different people on each project, managing stakeholder expectations and leading an entire project team to reach a desired goal, is a tremendous experience.

Q6• What do you think are the top issues that project managers face today?

It's all about interpersonal skills and dealing with different characteristics and cultures.

One of the main roles for project managers is to be able to manage cultural differences and avoiding conflicts, to lead the project team to success. Virtual teams have also been a challenge, where projects are being performed in different geographic regions. Another issue, is the challenges of project team members having to work in a matrix organization. This usually creates confusion for the project team members to balance the priorities of the project manager and their functional manager. Having to report to two bosses can be challenging, and ultimately can impact the functional and project performance.

Q7• Do you think there is a stereotype attached to project managers?

Stereotypes exist, such as project managers not being considered technical enough to judge the quality of outcomes and services rendered by functional teams. Another stereotype is that, project managers are project accountants. Yes, one of a project manager's responsibilities is to control the project budget and costs, however, this is not their sole concern. Time, quality and the project delivering its intended benefits, are also of high importance to a project manager.

Q8• Why is it important to celebrate international women's day?

March 8th is celebrated worldwide as International Women's Day. It is a great occasion for every woman to celebrate her life successes, at home and at work, as well as to think about possible improvements.

Today men should be included as well in gender equity topics, particularly in the workplace, and should support women more than ever. Together we are stronger! Increased diversity, equates to greater creativity.

Q9• On international women' s day, what is the most important message you offer to project management professionals?

As a professional woman with over 14 years of experience and as a mother of a young daughter, I have always strived for work-life balance. This hasn't been easy, yet it was possible. I have managed teams with both female and male members, and it has been an amazing experience. Women are amazing multitaskers and generally are very committed. The key is to perform efficiently in whatever you do.

Getting what you want, takes a lot of perseverance, patience and focus on your long-term goals. So don't wait to be noticed, have courage, move forward and be proactive. Seek out mentors and build professional networks. Attend conferences and consider further education. Be visible and believe your contribution counts. Read a lot, write your own points of view and train your mind to be more analytical. Be an open-minded woman, who's up-to-date, with an analytical mind and strong leadership skills, by developing yourself as an individual and also within your organization.

Mona Fazel

Mona Fazel is a certified project management professional with over 14 years of hands-on experience in management and consulting while supporting multiple industries. Having worked on large scale projects and various people she has gained sound knowledge of project resources planning, budgeting, cost control and forecasting. Experienced in managing PMO and project teams by building and motivating team members to meet project goals, adhering to their responsibilities and project milestones.

Raji Sivaraman
Singapore

ASBA LLC / Principal

Q1• Describe your journey as a project management professional.

True to the aged old saying, project management is an "accidental profession!". That was indeed true for me too. I was in the process of getting a technical Information Technology certification in Dow Jones. A lady next to me was nervous about a pending exam she needed to take the next day. I asked her what exam she was going to take. She said PMP. I did not know what that was at that time and enquired about its details. The more I heard about it, the more I thought of myself this should be a piece of cake for me as I am already doing all of this in my personal and work life. A year later, I took the exam, then went on to do my Master of Science in Project Management, then got certified in as PMI-ACP, PMO-CP, and many more. Now, project management and agile are part of my academic career too as well as a practitioner. So I call myself a Pracademic.

Q2• Why did you choose to become a project management professional?

I will answer this question with a few questions!

- *Are you Empowering yourselves to manage project changes with agility?*
- *What is empowerment?*
- *Are you ready for the changes that drive your projects?*
- *Are you changing the way you change?*

These are some of the probing questions that prompted me to do something about, people, process and technology. That translated to project management, agile mindsets and many inspiring ways of dealing with change 360 degrees.

Being agile and how it takes you to your 'now' state and beyond. "The struggle you are in today is developing the strength you need for tomorrow" – quotes Robert Tew. This is exactly what project management and personal agility is to me - 'to take the now and go beyond'.

Project management aspects encompass a lot of emphasis on managing stakeholders, and this led to a fairly natural transition to the world of project management and agile for me actually. This is one of the reason I became the co-founder of Agility Discoveries (http://agilitydiscoveries.com/). Ipek Sahra had interviewed both of us on our work of the Personal Agility Light House (PALH™) model.

Q3• Have you encountered any related obstacles in advancing your career?

As I say in my book, "Making Projects Sing" (https://www.amazon.com/Making-Projects-Sing-Perspective-Management/dp/1631574590) project management is not just for Information Technology or construction. It is for every single discipline, which is why I wrote the book to show that music and project management go hand in hand. But getting the world to fathom this concept of using agile and project management in all of the different sectors, has been a hard sell. Another obstacle is the fact that I moved to stay in many different countries and that took a toll on my career as well. But being the agile person that I am, I learned new languages, cultures and fit myself into the shoes of the other as quickly as I can.

As it is, this is not a job for the weak-minded. Project Managers and agile practitioners have the unenviable job of getting many different stakeholders all on the same page, getting them aligned with scope requirements and quality requirements for the projects. If that doesn't happen, the project is going to fail. And no matter how powerful or educated we are as project managers or agile practitioners, we will never have all the power we need to resolve these conflicts between the needs and wants of different stakeholders for expectation management. We may be working with many stakeholders who outrank us; sponsors, customers, federal regulatory agencies, and the list is endless. So it's in a way a strategic endeavor too. Having said that, it's in my mind very rewarding if we can run a project successfully, meet the goals that we plan to meet, and create value for our company and all the stakeholders.

Q4• Why is it important that more people work in the project management area?

I think project management skills are tremendously important for professionals today and the younger generation especially to achieve better performance in a dynamic, competitive and complex environment. The task of the next generation of the project mangers are not just delivering KPI and financial matrices, but also to be professionals who can anticipate and navigate through some of the changing dynamics. As a reviewer/contributor of the book, Advances in

Analytics and Data Science - Aligning Business Strategies and Analytics: Bridging Between Theory and Practice, I saw this need for the Next Gen more closely. This hits closer to home, since I work with Gen Z as a professor of Strategic Project Management in the university and also as a Board Director heading the Youth Climate Award to be presented a the COP26 for WAFA with volunteers from 35 countries, led by my executive chair from Saudi Arabia.

Jobs are being outsourced and being automated in this tough economy. A project management job, cannot be automated, and there's a much smaller chance of your job being outsourced. The scarcity of these abilities makes them very high demand. Project management is now moving towards the agile mindsets and having the hybrid (agile plus traditional project management) approach. That is the quintessential food of project management and agile excellence.

Q5•   How can we encourage more people to pursue project management as a career?

As I said before organizations are downscaling, and getting rid of middle management. They are replacing them with project managers and agile practitioners who are filling in the emptiness. Therefore the Gen Z can be the perfect adhesive in my mind. Encouraging the next generation to be project managers, will mean that a paradigm shift needs to take place. This will then lead to including as much agile into the system as possible.

Some organizations have Chief Project Officers these days and that is probably an incentive -to see the career go to the C level. Disruption is the new norm, and as such impact is seen in collaborative and digital means of doing work. This warrants current project economy awareness to be the prime important direction to lead and encourage people to take project management as a career and the agility drivers of tomorrow.

Q6• What do you think are the top issues that project managers face today?

In an article titled "The Nurturing Side of a Project Manager", in Project Management Review magazine of China*, I had written that, I don't know if there is any proof to suggest that either gender make better project managers or agile practitioners. Nevertheless, possessing the full range of skills and abilities needed to be a project manager, regardless of gender, leads to the completion of successful projects within the constraints of any organization. Given the multi tempered environment and the ever fluctuating forces at work of this decade and the future, expectation management is I think, the top issue that is faced across the broad spectrum.

*http://www.pmreview.com.cn/english/Home/article/detail/id/354.html

Q7• Do you think there is a stereotype attached to project managers?

There is a typecast of the traditional "PMP" suit project manager. Someone who follows processes to the T, is more prescriptive and herding the sheep. The other side of the coin is the servant leader who is more of a coordinator for the project. That constitutes the Agilists. Ethnocentrism to a little extent, may be found. In some organizations project mangers are considered to be controllers, schedulers, coders and the list goes on. Then, there is the notion of project managers are for just construction, tech jobs etc. which is soon changing, which is a good turn of events.

Q8• Why is it important to celebrate international women's day?

Accelerating gender parity, anti-sexism etc were the genesis of the start of the celebration of this day in 1913 on the 8th of March. But some say the origin was a different date and year. Some also argue that the reason for celebration is lost to a extent in the recent era, as not women's rights and the battle for equality, but the women themselves are the current focus.

According to UN.org, the 2019 theme is, "Think equal, build smart, innovate for change", focusing on innovative ways women can advance gender equality and empowerment in terms of "social protection systems, access to public services and sustainable infrastructure".
https://www.nbcnews.com/better/lifestyle/what-international-women-s-day-why-does-it-still-matter-ncna980746

Q9•   On international women' s day, what is the most important message you offer to project management professionals?
To drive the change for global companies, the crucial ingredient for adopting, adapting and dealing with disruption is; to become as agile as you can. This does not mean that the waterfall, traditional approaches are not used. They are used and embedded within the agile systems. In short, using a hybrid approach will eliminate a lot of risks and difficulties in making projects a great success.

Being positive in personal capabilities - Hone bold attitudes - Support optimistic goals and ambitions - believe in yourself first, to make the internal and external stakeholders and the project teams to believe in themselves and the project -Always keep in mind, end to end transformation including agile transformation is key, not just the end result.

Raji Sivaman

Raji Sivaraman, M. S, PMI-ACP, PMP, PMO-CP, Principal of ASBA LLC, a Singapore citizen, helps USA/Singapore companies with strategic planning/overseas startups. Speaks several languages. Worked in Singapore, Thailand, India and the USA. Helps fortune 50/500 companies with CSR/BSR/Mobility projects. Consultant, Director, Strategic Advisor and an Advisory Board member for non-profit organizations. Worked in IT, publishing, financial, standards and logistics industries as a consultant, lead project manager and implementation manager. Adjunct Professor at Montclair University, USA. Researcher, Author, Contributor to Project Management books, published articles, research and white papers internationally. Global facilitator, keynote speaker, Discussant/Academic chair/Moderator CXO Forum and a panelist. An Agile practitioner with a Master of Science Degree in Project Management. Held workshops around the world. A mentor for various organizations, a Pracademic. Distinguished Women leaders of Singapore, 2013.

Ramesh Vahidi
United Kingdom

Southampton Business School / Senior Academic Programme Leader

Q1• Describe your journey as a project management professional.

My Project Management (PM) journey so far has had two distinctive, though interrelated parts. The first leg was being a PM professional for several years, the second started with becoming an academic, developing the new generation of project professionals, hopefully responsible ones.

I was lucky enough that my career started in a project environment right after graduating as an Industrial Engineer. This followed by working with five other project companies or parts of large organisations that were run by projects. The companies were active in strategic planning, executive education, heavy industries, power industry, management consulting, system design and industrial research. The roles varied from system analyst, project engineer, senior analyst to project manager and consultant in a variety of projects and programmes such as; national strategic planning, executive education, designing IT master plans and opportunity study for large industrial investments to name a few.

During those years, I frequently consulted PM books and handbooks when we faced minor or major issues in projects (in parallel with working on them) to see what they would suggest. These were mainly books published before 2006, which dominantly focused on scheduling, budgeting and resource allocation. This meant they had rarely assigned a full chapter or even small sections to soft aspects of PM, such as stakeholders management, leadership, strategic management or project.

The more I read, the more I found them detached from the realities of projects we were dealing with on a daily basis. Then, it happened that as part of some IT projects, I had to run training sessions for senior users and managers. This was an interesting experience and seemed very rewarding in terms of increasing user engagement, awareness and building rapport to ensure higher acceptance level of the project outcome.

Combination of such experiences and the gaps in the PM academic knowledge became a turning point in my career. I decided to return to academia for further studies in PM mainly to do research with pragmatic value which could reflect the real challenges. Joining the academia to study International Project Management, soon led to further studies and an academic career in PM. Today, I am leading a Master's in PM, which was designed following and based on the in-depth research on decision-making and trade-offs in projects during my PhD. Overall, the journey has been a learning curve blending management, consultancy, education and research in Project Management.

Q2•   Why did you choose to become a project management professional?

In answering your previous question, I should have stated my career trajectory started from way before I even know what project management was. This is practicing my pitch in the classroom, where we discuss everyone has managed loads of things with project characteristics since their childhood. So, I would go back to those days. Since I remember, I used to enjoy making various artifacts and had a strong preference for doing unique things with special outcome rather than routine and repeating tasks for the same and predefined/fully expected outcome. Indeed, I have always been busy doing things with project characteristics and creating something new in my own time.

Regarding the professional life, as my initial degrees were in Industrial Engineering, with Operations Research (known as the root of the traditional PM), a career in projects seemed one of the natural routes. So, PM was a very close match professionally and personally.

Q3•   Have you encountered any related obstacles in advancing your career?

I was lucky enough in projects to work with a few very supportive managers who most valued and appreciated your commitment to work, competencies and hard-work over anything else. They indeed, paved the way for me to push the boundaries and to take on more responsibilities in some large projects and programmes. These were despite being among the few, or the only female, in most of the projects and environments I used to work in. The project teams were also very supportive and collaborative, so we overcame many obstacles and prevented new ones to take over.

Q4•   Why is it important that more people work in the project management area?

There is a common belief based on the real world evidences that organisations (generally societies) are increasingly moving towards using projects to manage their businesses. Published research and PM professional bodies' reports have also been indicating the need for more project professionals.

To elaborate, further to a need for more people in the PM area, I believe we need more people in non-project jobs to learn about projects, as well. This would enable them to communicate, collaborate and work more effectively with project professionals. This is part of my introduction to any PM module that some of the cohort might not necessary wish or end up being a project professional, set aside a project manager. However, they will inevitably end up working alongside project professionals or being affected by projects one way or another. So, PM knowledge is an essential tool in anybody's toolbox!

Q5• How can we encourage more people to pursue project management as a career?

By introducing them to the area, its attractiveness, inevitable challenges and difficulties and its impact in their lives and organisations. This could happen in schools (as professional bodies have been promoting the profession for a while) or various organisations. Further, to people who find projects and project environments right matches for their personalities and competencies, so persuade it as a profession, we should also encourage those who feel more comfortable in non-project roles, learn what PM is all about, so that they could work comfortably alongside project professionals when need be.

Q6• What do you think are the top issues that project managers face today?

I would respond this with my both hats on, as a former project manager and as an academic. My main and overarching concern has been distinguishing between what will work and what will not in project and who to listen to for these.

A quick search of the social media and the big (and profitable) market of 'PM-related knowledge and services', will show you extremely different views on projects and how they should be managed. There are plenty of books, blogs, articles and so on, that confidently suggest you guaranteed success, in any project by following their suggested few simple tips and steps (normally in shiny and colorful graphs!).

In the meantime, ask highly experienced project managers that what it takes to deal with complexities of managing projects and how far they could confidently guarantee success of a project despite all their efforts and good intentions. Evidenced with the project experiences, my previous research and continued conversations with PM professionals, I would doubt, they make such promises that a simple and straightforward recipe for any projects success exist or would 100% work. If there were, organisations with multi-million pound/dollar projects would have followed the steps for years and years, and we did not have any failed projects!

Many of the claims with commercial purposes create a simplistic illusion that somebody has the solution for all your project problems, undermining the hard work it takes to become an effective project professional and manage a project. On the other hand, given the pressures of the fast moving world around us, simple and fast solutions are becoming more popular to some (fortunately not all yet!). Hence, my constant worry is for those new to PM who buy into such ideas and learn the reality in hard ways; set aside the damage to organisations, ultimately societies, these could cause. So, having PM professionals and academics, who are committed to responsible conduct and would be able to distinguish such illusions and intentions from realities of what it takes to manage project are among the top issues, from where I stand.

Q7• Do you think there is a stereotype attached to project managers?

This is a very good question! I am not aware of a common stereotype but would certainly keep an eye and investigate to learn if and what they are!

Q8• Why is it important to celebrate international women's day?

Not the easiest question, indeed! On the day, women's achievements are celebrated and various events attempt to raise awareness and call for action on gender equality. All for invaluable reasons and causes as undeniably, we have still a long way to go.

However, I wish one's achievements as a female, were basically perceived as a human achievement without paying attention or even thinking what their gender is or marking one day on our calendars (out of 365) for the past hundred years (since the Day was introduced) to remember these.

Q9• On international women' s day, what is the most important message you offer to project management professionals?

Let's carefully and constantly watch our words, acts, thoughts and perceptions, during projects' difficulties or celebration of achievements,

*to see whether any of our judgements and decisions might
(intentionally or unintentionally) reflect a bias towards people's gender
or could be interpreted as such.*

*Looking back at the project, evaluate how such biased judgements
could have or had possibly motivated or demotivate the team
members, affected their well-being and consequently affected the
project. True (self-) reflections followed by small corrective actions
would gradually build up an unbiased culture, which benefit the
individuals, the project and ultimately the whole organisation. Let's all
win together!*

Ramesh Vahidi

*Ramesh designed and has been leading the MSc in Project
Management (PM) at Southampton Business School since 2012. She
has taught PM and supervised at postgraduate, PhD and
undergraduate levels since 2008.*

*Following her initial degrees in Industrial Engineering (Iran University
of Technology and Sharif University of technology, Iran), she took a
number of roles in projects and programme environments, including
project management, senior analyst, exec trainer and consultant in a
few major companies and organisations in various industries.*

*She returned to academia in 2006 to explore pragmatic PM theories,
which led to an MSc and a PhD in PM (Chalmers University, Sweden
and Northumbria University, UK). Her main aim and passion have
remained integrating PM theories to the actual practice through
teaching and research with pragmatic values. Her PhD research on
'Conceptual framework for trade-off decisions in projects' was granted*

one of the first PhD awards of the Major Projects Association (MPA) for its impact on the practice of major projects.

Ramesh's main research areas are making of critical decisions and trade-offs in projects; ethical decision-making in PM (a team research sponsored and published by PMI); work-life balance in project environments; responsible management/ PM education and generally critical analysis of PM theories. She has been working voluntarily with APM and PMI for a couple of years in different capacities, i.e. local committee member, researcher, grant proposal/paper reviewer and speaker. She has extensively presented in international conferences, including IPMA, EDEN, CIB, AHP, PRME to name a few and has also delivered CPD events for PMI on Decision Making for PMI UK and was a panel member and presenter at the MPA Wellbeing event. Ramesh is also a qualified performance coach. She also presents artwork at exhibitions and conferences.

Ruth Pearce
USA

ALLE LLC / President

Project Motivator / CEO

Q1• Describe your journey as a project management professional.

I became a project manager when I was an IT developer. I was on a pilot project in NYC and the project manager had to return home to the UK unexpectedly. The choice was to have me, a person whom the client already knew, take over as the project manager and replace me as the developer with someone from the UK or to replace the project manager with someone, who did not know the client or the project. It was decided that relationship building was key and that I would step into the project manager role. I had no prior experience – although many people saw me as organized!

The key was that the organization and the client believed that the tools and processes of project could be learned, and that there was no substitute for established relationships and trust.

Q2• Why did you choose to become a project management professional?

Initially I did not choose it. I thought, I wanted to be an economist at a stockbroker. I studied Economics at the University of Bath and then a Masters at the London School of Economics. After a few months it became clear that my image of the role was not the reality and I took and passed an aptitude test in computing. I thought, I would work in development or QA.

The opportunity to try out as a project manager came up on the project in New York and I found that I loved it – at least the way I practiced it. I focused on relationship building and networking, getting the input from as many people as possible, communicating in different ways with different audiences. Once I had tried it, project management seemed like the natural fit for me. The variety in the projects and the organizations I worked for over the years, stimulated my curiosity. The smart people I had the opportunity to work with and the opportunity to work alongside people from many cultures and backgrounds satisfied my appreciation of beauty, excellence and my love of learning and also leveraged my strength of fairness. I was grateful for the opportunity to be a facilitator of the success of others. That is how I have always seen project management – being the facilitation of the success of others.

Q3• Have you encountered any related obstacles in advancing your career?

Over the years I have found it can be a challenge to challenge. Sometimes when we, as project managers come into possession of data and information that suggest that a change is needed or a project is not worth continuing with, there is resistance. It can be hard to overcome the commitment others have to prior decisions. In economic theory, I learned "let bygones be bygones" and "don't send good money after bad". At any point in time it is OK to re-evaluate based on new information and data and change course. However, turning a large project or program can be like turning the Titanic and for project managers successfully changing or canceling a project, is not typically regarded as being a successful project manager!

Another challenge is overcoming our own and others' biases. As humans, we look for data that supports our underlying beliefs (confirmation bias), we are overly optimistic about the time it takes to get things done (planning bias) and we dwell on negative experiences over positive ones (negativity bias). The first one makes it hard to change course or consider a new idea, the second means that we habitually underestimate the time, expense and effort required to complete a project, and the last means that stakeholders tend to overstress failures and setbacks, and are less able to appreciate the opportunities that arise from experimentation and occasional failure.

And while I have not faced any particular challenges as a female project manager, I have faced challenges being a woman in the workplace – especially when I was young and looked to people to mentor and guide me.

Q4• Why is it important that more people work in the project management area?

I am not sure that it is as important that more people work in the project management area, as it is important that we appreciate the strengths – and limitations – of project managers, challenge some of the stereotypes such as that project managers are thwarted by lack of authority or that they are micromanagers of tasks. We can benefit by increasing the skills of project managers to incorporate basic leadership principles, to build social intelligence and to make connecting with stakeholders and team members the core of our profession. We are leaders focused on a set of time-bound outcomes rather than leaders focused on operational, repeated activities.

We also benefit when we understand better the workings of the human brain; how we make decisions, how to challenge habitual thinking and how to make planning more rational.

Q5•   How can we encourage more people to pursue project management as a career?
I think the biggest thing is to remove the notion that being a project manager means NOT being something else. It is not either or. My most satisfying roles have been those where I have been both the project manager AND a contributor to the final product or service. They have also been the roles where I learned a great deal!

There is research that shows that many organizations regard project managers who are also producers of the project output as preferable to people who just concentrate on the mechanics of a project's tasks. We tend to be more interested; we encourage better decision-making, we keep an eye on the big picture, and we help others to prioritize and produce.

Another way to appeal to people, so that they treat project management as a worthy and useful skill is to create apprenticeships. This is a doing and being profession. It is not so much about getting certified or passing an exam. It is about learning how to be nimble at the moment, responsive to issues, open to ideas and to develop methods to challenge assumptions. A great way to do that, is to work alongside someone who has developed those faculties.

Another opportunity that I am passionate about, is to create group coaching opportunities, where small groups of project management professionals can explore everyday challenges, examine the strengths they have to meet those challenges and to understand where they need the help of others.

Seeing a group of people share experiences, explore challenges and help each other to create a path forward is very rewarding and helps them to feel less isolated and more connected. There is great value in having a group who is in your corner and you are in theirs.

Helping people to build connection and community, showing that project management is a collaborative activity will help attract people to it – whether as their full-time role or as part of another role that they play in their organization.

The more team members there are who understand the value of project management and how to put it into practice, the easier it is to manage a successful project!

Q6• What do you think are the top issues that project managers face today?
That is a tough question because I think different people in different domains experience their own challenges.

One issue is the difference – or similarity – between change management and project management. Understanding how they overlap and our role in managing change, winning over hearts and minds, is key.

Another challenge is the complexity of our current environment. Things move fast, there is constant pressure to be available and to deliver. A good project manager creates space for their team. We all need space, downtime, rejuvenation so a good project manager builds that into the day for them and for their team members.

Fear of change, fear of what AI will replace – maybe it will replace us?

I believe that with more automation and increased dependence on AI, the skills we have as project managers in connecting with others, to their strengths, their desires, communicating with sensitivity and clarity, understanding the way in which humans naturally process information and make decisions become more and more important. We have a great deal of opportunity to make project management count.

I love the work by Carole Osterweil that she covers in her book, Project Delivery, Uncertainty and Neuroscience: A Leader's Guide to Walking in Fog.

I am also a huge fan of the work that Joshua Ramirez and Jodi Bull Wilson are doing at the Institute of Neuro- & Behavioral Project Management (NBPMI) that looks at biases and decision-making. They are creating a model of project management process that fully integrates our current understanding of the brain.

Q7• Do you think there is a stereotype attached to project managers?

I actually did some research on this very question – asking project management professionals and their colleagues about their impression of project managers. While many people in the survey agreed that project managers are needed for projects to succeed, it was interesting that a large majority of respondents – both project managers and their colleagues – have a perception of project managers being micro managers, planning too many meetings with the wrong people in the room, taking up time with excessive process and in that way, getting in the way of progress.

The age-old stereotype of project managers with clip boards checking off tasks is still with us in some places.

Often project managers and PMOs are seen as process managers and tactical resources, and they are not woven into the organizational decision-making process as they could be. They are not positioned to define, support and advance organizational strategy.

Another preconception is that project managers DRIVE projects that they are somehow responsible for energizing people to get the work done. That is a big responsibility and can be a thankless task. When we connect with the core motivators of our stakeholders and team members – their why and with who they are – we cultivate a collaborative and collegian environment and don't have to drive at all!

Q8• Why is it important to celebrate international women's day?

It is important to focus peoples' attention on those who are doing good work. International Women's Day is a way to focus attention on what women around the world are doing. Some of the most powerful stories are about women who come from cultures where there is little, or no semblance of equality and those stories show what is possible. International Women's Day also highlights the progress that has taken place and the progress we still need to make.

Hearing other's stories is inspiring to the rest of us.

Q9• On international women' s day, what is the most important message you offer to project management professionals?

The message that every change begins with you. If you want others to be more engaged, be more engaged yourself. If you want others to be brave, be brave yourself. If you want others to be strong, show the strengths in you. If you want others to be hopeful, be hopeful yourself – not just being optimistic but identifying the steps to move forward. If you want others to listen, listen yourself. If you want others to be curious and open, be open and curious yourself, be ready to learn about things outside your immediate domain.

Be Hopeful; Be Strong; Be Brave; Be Curious

Ruth Pearce

Ruth brings over 25 years of experience in the field of project management in the domains of financial services, state government, education and non-profits. She is also an experienced group coach, author, speaker and trainer.

She holds the position of Product & Practice Development Consultant at the VIA Institute Character and Certified Coach Trainer at the Center for Coaching Certification.

Her core competencies are in bringing the research and practices of positive psychology - in particular character strengths - to the workplace through training and coaching. She loves to share the best evidence-based tools and methods with her followers. Ruth has spoken to more than 20,000 people in more than 45 countries about the topic of Social Intelligence for Project Leaders and loves to study character strengths use among project managers to better understand how they can grow in influence and success. She is also a student of mindfulness and loves to explore how increased mindfulness increases productivity, reduces implicit biases and improves decision-making.

Her book Be a Project Motivator: Unlock the Secrets of Strengths-Based Project Management was published in 2018. Later this year she will be launching a course in the Foundations of Social Intelligence for Project Managers (FoSI4PMs) as well as a Mindfulness Based Strengths Practice for Project Managers (MBSP4PMs) and Coaching Skills for Professional Project Managers (CS4PPMs).

Sandy Lawrence
USA

Monster Smart / Owner

Q1• Describe your journey as a project management professional.

I've always had a penchant for working tasks in front of me to completion; but am also keen to keeping my head up and constantly looking at the horizon to capture what is happening around me. I found great opportunities harnessing this strength early in my career as a management consultant with two Big 4 consulting firms. I developed an appreciation for companies and groups that were innovative and built my own company through a relationship I had established years ago in the Utility industry. My grass-roots company gave me opportunities to learn all aspects of running a business, from software development to marketing, finance, and staffing. Every customer project created multiple internal projects to handle such as customer inquiries, billing issues, product delivery, etc. Most importantly, I learned how to listen to customers' requirements to ensure we built products that were useful and usable. After achieving my Masters in Curriculum and Technology, I used this new knowledge to move into a more formal training and project management role. This led me to opportunities in the Federal, State, and law enforcement arenas. In 2005, I signed up for a project that required a secret-level security clearance, which kick-

started the last 10 years of my career in the military environment. During the time from 2005 on, I acquired my 3 PMI credentials, PMP, PgMP, and PfMP. Working as a Department of defense (DoD) contractor I was able to utilize my PMI certifications and build 3 PMOs, establish governance, work to build and execute an Information Technology (IT) Strategic Plan, and a Portfolio Management System. My career has given me the opportunity to shape lives through the creation of the Military Liaison Program that I started through PMI and is now formally recognized in over 60 US and Canada chapters. I am also a speaker and co-author of books on transition in project management, IT, Logistics, and Cybersecurity.

Q2• Why did you choose to become a project management professional?

After selling my company of 12 years, I realized I should re-engineer myself and highlight my skills that I accumulated during my consulting contracts and owning my own company to get back into the workforce to build a new career. Up to this time, all my work had been in IT-related activities. I researched project management and found it was a career that would allow me to continue working the way I work, in potentially any industry I wanted. The PMP was the best way to exhibit the expertise I wanted to share and be recognized for; it was also the most prominent 'preferred' skill on most job descriptions. After acquiring my Masters in Education, I also chose to formally accentuate my passion and interest in Project Management. The local PMI chapter was offering local exam prep classes which is how I prepared myself for the PMP.

Q3• Have you encountered any related obstacles in advancing your career?

I would say that I did not encounter obstacles, but more of a set of limiting factors in advancing my career. These included the inability to travel 80 to 100% of my time during my Big 4 experience, as I started my family at that same time. Another factor was in the realm of ethics – I resigned from some very prosperous jobs because of the unethical behavior by my senior management. They were hard decisions at the time, but I slept well at night knowing that any more time invested in the job would be disastrous. I sought to seize all opportunities utilizing my contacts network, my knowledge of how various industries operate and my passion for project management, all yielding a wonderful career journey that has taken me to places I'd never thought possible.

Q4• Why is it important that more people work in the project management area?

It gives one a broader perspective on many levels. Project Management is a team effort. It offers humility; when you fail at your first project, when you have difficulty influencing other people to work, when you simply do not know everything you need to know, you learn to surround yourself with smart people and ask for help. It also offers an understanding of servant leadership, and that you are not the nucleus of all that there is. Project Management helps one learn team building, coaching, communication, managing self and others, servant leadership, and much more.

Q5• How can we encourage more people to pursue project management as a career?

Communicating this reality has been my passion for the last 6 years! I became known at the Military Commands where I worked as the "PMP Girl". Given my 3 credentials, I was working on architecting and executing both portfolio systems and strategic planning efforts and had direct access to the CIO, Deputy CIO, CTO and Senior Leaders of all

IT Directorates. Many veterans were interested in learning more about project management, and I offered my time and personal experience to help answer questions and became a coach to many on how to achieve the PMP. Individual requests turned into lunch-n-learns to share with groups of 20, 30 or more. The person's interest and commitment was there, but it was hard to find anyone unified source for military members to go to besides myself. One of my favorite success stories stems from an opportunity I had working with an Army Lieutenant Colonel who I coached on attaining his PMP. We discovered we shared an interest in helping others, and together, worked on 2 major efforts in our spare time; first of which was co-authoring a book for transitioning military on how to assess and get a commercial job in project management. At the same time, we worked on a grass-roots effort to get a Military Liaison Program we had created at our local PMI chapter recognized by corporate PMI and standardized for all U.S. chapters. I am happy to say that PMI has formally recognized and instituted the Military Liaison Program and offers this program in over 70 chapters in the U.S. and Canada! In retrospect, people saw my passion towards being a PMP champion and were intrigued enough to ask me about my credentials and how to follow in my footsteps. As a result, I decided to lead by example and help change lives for the better by helping others seeking professional careers in project management.

Q6• What do you think are the top issues that project managers face today?

I believe one of the biggest issues facing project managers today is to adequately assess and understand what a company is looking for in their project managers, and help them mature along this path. Not all companies use project managers well; and with the continual discussion around traditional versus agile project management, companies get lost in knowing what they need. Additionally, the certification market for project managers is bloated with certification frenzy, especially in the agile arena. Who knows what to acquire? My advice is to stick with organizations that have certifications that are worldwide known and are used as requirements in job descriptions. For example, PMI statistically has the most references of their certifications in job descriptions as seen in the large online search engines. Another issue is that the project management career field has exploded over the last 30 years with the advent of technology; this explosion has created great job opportunities for project managers worldwide. Most companies know they need project managers, but are not fully aware of the insight, knowledge, and corporate understanding a project manager can offer to help beyond projects and programs. I think it is tough for some to quickly determine the maturity of the organization, leadership's goals, and what actually makes the organization tick. Having the ability to recognize these key items and know how to help the organization be successful can, in turn, help project managers can climb to program managers, to portfolio managers, to PMO managers, and to key executive level positions. Similarly, one must have the ability to keep a finger on the pulse of the organization regarding strategic objectives and associated market influences, as well as understanding their direct alignment to corporate goals.

Q7• Do you think there is a stereotype attached to project managers?

I learned through my PMI leadership efforts that there are many types of people in project management; most like to lead, some are very good at group consensus, some are great at research and capturing statistics to support an important decision. Some are good at all of these. The key is to be aware of the expertise and knowledge around you. As project management is grounded in process and technology, most of us were technology geeks. When speaking about career paths of project managers, I caution people to consider the transition from technical expert to management. This can cause many people frustration and lead to failure. Project managers must be very cognizant of their communication skills, as they need to speak in the language of the person or audience they are speaking with, i.e., technical experts or senior leadership. Project managers must be acutely aware of what every group wants from the project and in what form of communication they operate with; one of the most critical skills to acquire and perform well.

Q8• Why is it important to celebrate international women's day?

It is exciting to see corporations in particular recognize women's accomplishments, not only in project management arenas, but successes in all their endeavors. Project Management transcends industries, and women employing their natural "multi-tasking" management skills have greater opportunities to make a real difference and be acknowledged for all their achievements and accolades they so richly deserve! The more women we see in these roles, especially in international settings, the more inspired others will be!

Q9• On international women' s day, what is the most important message you offer to project management professionals?

During my time as an Advisor to the PMI EMEA Leadership Institute Master Class, I became acutely aware that project managers have the same goals, aspirations, drive and passion for this wonderful career field, no matter what country you are from. You can travel the world and work anywhere and find a kinship in the pursuit of greatness in project management. It is up to you to continuously expand your network, use organizations like PMI to reach out and participate to expand this career field. Don't hesitate to ask questions to better understand your role and how you can best succeed, and take pride in what you accomplish and what you can do to help others to accomplish through collective efforts.

Sandy Hoalth Lawrence

Sandy Lawrence has delivered powerful results in more than 5 diverse industries, from start-up organizations to mature corporations, Federal Agencies, and military commands for the better part of four decades. Currently, semi-retired, Sandy works as an author, instructor, consultant, and a willing contributor of expertise when it comes to helping people, start-ups, and structured organizations transform and transition in order to reach and exceed their goals. Her volunteer focus has been primarily with the Project Management Institute (PMI), where she has been a member for over 15 years serving at both the local chapter and global levels; she holds the Emeritus Board position at the PMI Chapter of Tampa Bay. Certifications include the PfMP, PgMP, PMP, as well as the Lean Six Sigma green belt and ITIL certifications. Sandy graduated from the PMI Leadership Institute Master Class in 2011; in 2012, she was honored to be the LIMC Advisor for the EMEA class.

Sandy has held many positions through PMI and at the local chapter, from being on the team to establish the PfMP exam and evaluation process, to writing exam questions, standards and guides. She also evaluates and recommends presentations for US and EMEA Conferences, and works as a narrative evaluator for both the PgMP and PfMP application exams.

Sandy's passion and appreciation for the military gave cause for her to write and co-publish four books aimed at helping military members transition into the corporate workforce. She dedicated her free time to launch a grass-roots effort within PMI to recognize and launch the Military Liaison Program – helping military in their quest for project management careers and knowledge. Sandy says she's honored that this effort has resulted in PMI Global to formally endorse and offer the Military Liaison Program in over 60 PMI chapters in the US and Canada.

Teresa Knudson
USA

Mayo Clinic/ Senior Director

Q1• Describe your journey as a project management professional.

Each person's journey into project management is different. It typically isn't one that you select when you are at the university but is one that you are attracted to over time as you are presented with various career opportunities to lead projects. That is exactly how my journey into project management began.

As an aspiring young professional, I was interested in learning new things and willing to take on different roles within my organization. My initial role in management was in an area that was going through a major system implementation being lead a team of organizational leaders. Being new to the area and my role, I was not part of this major project but watched from the sidelines until one day I was asked to manage a team to define data configuration requirements by bringing a diverse team together. Unfortunately, the overall project was struggling to meet deadlines and demonstrate results so as a "last resort", my supervisor asked me to step in as the project manager. Obviously, I was totally unprepared, untrained, and unaware of what I was getting into but with my background in business, finance and information technology I was going to give it my best to figure it out. That's where I learned the basics about project management through hard work and a lot of heroic efforts by an amazing group of people.

Needless to say, after that experience I was hooked. The sense of teamwork and accomplishment was tremendous – especially realizing that we had achieved something for our organization that had never been done before and would actually last 30 years!

I went onto another managerial role from there but was soon called upon to manage another major project that was having some issues. This one was, of course, bigger and more complex than the other one, so I needed to step up my game and my skills. As we were completing this project, I was asked again by leadership to lead another one. It was while I was in this third project that I noticed a trend, each time I was involved in these projects I was needing to start from scratch and there was no common approach or agreement on how to do project management.

When questioning our external consulting partner on this, they shared some information on "project portfolio management" with me and I knew I had found the answer. After more research into this and realizing the wealth of information, training, certifications and expertise that existed; I proposed the creation of an Enterprise Project and Portfolio Management Office (EPMO) for our organization. It's now been 12 years since this area was established and the organization has matured significantly during this time with all projects actively being tracked, over 300 Project Management Professionals (PMP) certified and managing all major projects, and leadership recognizing the importance and value of this profession in strategic execution. It's been quite a journey so far but there is always more to go as projects

163

continue to become bigger and more complex, technology advances at record pace, and organizations are needing to move and change faster than ever before.

Q2• Why did you choose to become a project management professional?

My situation is one where the profession chose me more than I chose the profession. Being trained in Business, Finance and Information Technology; this was not the path I originally planned on but has been one that I have thoroughly enjoyed. As I was provided with opportunities during my career to manage various projects, I embraced the challenge, valued the teamwork, and was thrilled by the sense of accomplishment.

I believe that it takes a special person to be a project manager. You need to be fearless and able to deal with the unknown while leading a team that questions you but, most importantly, needs you to support and encourage them.

Q3• Have you encountered any related obstacles in advancing your career?

Every career has obstacles and challenges. In project management one of the main ones for many of us has been the lack of understanding of what project management actually is and the wide range of skills necessary to be successful in this role. This is where the Project Management Institute (PMI) and the PMP has been tremendously valuable by learning the full range of skills involved has expanded the understanding and redefined it as a critical profession.

While the majority of leaders who have been involved in major projects, understand the role and the critical value it plays, there are still some who consider it "operational" rather than realizing the true strategic value of this position in an organization. As we all know, a strategic plan is just a bunch of ideas unless there is a project manager and a dedicated team doing the hard work of making it a reality.

Q4• Why is it important that more people work in the project management area?

Everyone of us needs to have project management as a core skill in whatever we do. This is necessary in both our personal and professional lives to make anything happen successfully. Whether remodeling your kitchen or implementing a multi-million dollar computer system, project management skills are needed. Obviously, like other skills there is a wide spectrum of abilities and as you gain more experience and training your ability to take on larger and more difficult projects increases. I highly recommend these skills for all people as I've found these amazingly valuable and have gained the best experiences in my personal life in keeping things organized while working full time, raising three children, and taking care of the number of other things that life brings.

Q5• How can we encourage more people to pursue project management as a career?

My recommendation to all people interested in continually learning, building their skills, and advancing their careers; is to pursue opportunities in project management as an absolute requirement.

These skills clearly demonstrate your ability to take on challenges, to work with various types of people, and to actively solve problems while focusing on the end goal. Besides, there is nothing more rewarding than being part of a team that has accomplished something that is special and of value to others!

165

Q6. **What do you think are the top issues that project managers face today?**

The top issues facing project management, is actually similar to the issues facing many other professions. The world is moving faster than ever with rapidly changing technology, multiple communication channels, and the need to get things done more quickly. This is actually where project management has an advantage – who better to get things organized, create a plan, and get things done by working with others and continually building skills while taking on these issues directly.

Q7. **Do you think there is a stereotype attached to project managers?**

If there is still a stereotype attached to project managers, it's by people who have never really managed a project and therefore have no true understanding of the advanced management skills necessary in this profession. At the same time, it's also important for project managers to realize that their skills must go well beyond the tactical and technical components of the role, but also need to incorporate a full range of leadership skills, and a broad understanding of the business environment to truly be fully reflective of the profession and the position.

Q8. **Why is it important to celebrate international women's day?**

It is tremendously important to celebrate international women's day to serve as an example for the generations coming after us of the progress that has been made with women in the workplace and in leadership roles over the years. While much has been accomplished in the past, I'm sure we would all agree that there is still much more that needs to change for women to truly be in an equitable position with men in the workplace, at home, and within our government.

This day is a recognition and celebration of those that have come before us and whose effort and sacrifices have provided us with the opportunities that we enjoy today, but it is also a challenge to those that come after us to someday make this world a place where there is full gender equity and the need for this day no longer exists.

Q9• On international women' s day, what is the most important message you offer to project management professionals?

My message to project management professionals and to any woman in any profession is to have the confidence in your abilities to take on any challenge by making the commitment to yourself to be your best and always keep learning and evolving, meeting new people, and experiencing new adventures. Life goes by way too quickly so make the absolute most of every day.

Teresa Knudson

Teresa (Terri) Knudson is the Senior Director of Strategy Management Services (SMS) within the Department of Laboratory Medicine and Pathology at the Mayo Clinic. SMS is responsible for providing the full spectrum of strategy services to one of the largest departments in the organization from planning to execution to value delivery. Prior to this role Terri created and lead the Enterprise Portfolio Management Office (EPMO) which is responsible for managing the organizations portfolio, methodology and standards, education and skills development, project resourcing and consulting, system and support services, and analysis and reporting.

Terri has worked in various departments throughout Mayo Clinic including Strategic Planning Services, Finance, Information Technology, Internal Audit Services, Patient Financial Services, and Operations Administration. During these assignments she led some of the largest projects at Mayo Clinic.

Terri has a Masters' of Business Administration and Bachelors' Degrees in Accounting and Computer Science. She is a Certified Public Accountant, a Project Management Professional (PMP), a Program Management Professional (PgMP), and a Portfolio Management Professional (PfMP). Terri is also certified in Change Management and has Bronze and Silver Quality Awards.

Prior to joining Mayo Clinic, Terri held positions at Deloitte and Cenex. Terri is an active member of the Project Management Institute and currently serves on the PMI Board of Directors in addition to publishing, speaking, and consulting.

Vanita Bhoola (Dr.)

India

S.P. Jain Institute of Management & Research / Associate Professor &

Head of Executive Education and Centre for Project Management

Q1• Describe your journey as a project management professional.

My journey in the world of Project management started about 18 years ago. The initial phase was only teaching Post-Graduate students of Business Administration. I was simultaneously enrolled for PhD program – though the initial progress was slow due to high teaching load at SPJIMR. It was indeed a struggle to strike the right balance between research, teaching and some amount of academic administration during my early years at SPJIMR. SPJIMR has been growing with increasing requirements of administration, teaching and executive training in Project Management. I embraced the challenge! Eventually, as I was approaching completion of my PhD, I not only started teaching across all programs at SPJIMR, but also emerged as a researcher, publishing papers in "A" category international journals and reputed magazines. Conducting corporate training and handholding executives and project managers have always been by force. This was also the time when my daughter needed attention for her studies, as she was growing up. It was indeed a tightrope walk!

In 2012, I was entrusted with the responsibility of taking charge of the Centre of Project Management, at SPJIMR. In two years, I was able to turnaround the Centre and positive revenue inflows. At that time, I was at the verge of completion of my PhD with already a bunch of international publications, including "A" rated journals. Life was certainly not easy with dual responsibilities at office and home. There have been times when I just felt like giving up. Thank God, I have an extremely supporting family – especially, my mother-in-law.

In the year 2016, an additional responsibility came to me – managing the Centre for Management Development Programs (MDP) at SPJIMR! I have never shrugged away from responsibility. So, when it came, I gracefully accepted it, not clearly knowing what's in store.

By far, it was a greatest challenge! There were sharks out there! There were entities eagerly waiting and watching me to fail. But I couldn't fail – at least in the eyes of my daughter! I am her role model.

I realized that I need a unique strategy to manage all these activities. While there were things where I was indispensable – like teaching and research, I started gradually delegating responsibility after building a very efficient team. I used the concepts of critical thinking at workplace. Considered the work conditions and employee-employer relation as the "base", I tried to create a "superstructure" based on the lines of critical thinking that can redefine the work culture, roles and responsibilities.

I call it the ABCER model of critical thinking to facilitate shared leadership within my team. Using this model of critical thinking process flow I have been able to delegate considerable workload to a set of responsible colleagues who take complete ownership of work, thereby minimizing my intervention on a day-to-day supervision. My team uses this sequence as follows: Analyze (analyze the project problem, define project requirements, identify gaps, recognize project risks and recognize the cost-benefit dynamics) - Build (create performance measurement tools for team, connect to the thought-process and vibrations of stakeholders within the organization and clients/vendors, introduce equal-partnership and stake, instill a sense of ownership) - Connect (make them see your dream, enable free-flow of communication, introduce MIS/process maps, etc.) - Execute (discuss and resolve hurdles to execute work effectively, ensure quadruple constraints, help members identify and assess important insights, demonstrate ownership and leadership) - Replicate (once a project is executed, formulate processes to ensure smooth replication under similar conditions and with modifications/deviations) (ABCER). This model also ensures documentation of knowledge gained while executing any action, big or small. This enables future replication that can happen independent of the current person executing it.

Q2• Why did you choose to become a project management professional?

Currently, I divide my time between teaching, research, training and hand-holding practitioners. One complements the other. In 2012, when I was assigned the responsibility of the Centre of Project Management at SPJIMR, it was a loss-making department. It took me two years to turn around the department. As the Centre was attaining stability, I was assigned with another responsibility – this time it was bigger! It was the Centre of Management Development Program. Initially, I was not sure whether it was a punishment or reward (smiling… this is a mild joke).

This was the time I realized that managing two premium departments of a Business School that ranks among the top 5 national, is possible only with a magic wand!

Q3• Have you encountered any related obstacles in advancing your career?

Maintaining such a portfolio in an academic institution like SPJIMR, one of the top five Business Schools in India, with international accreditations and rankings like QS Global, AMBA and AACSB, is not easy. In fact, the volume of business at the MDP and CPM centers has increased by more than threefold in the past 3 years, since I have taken charge. In order to implement shared leadership in an academic institution with a corporate work culture, systems and processes are of critical importance. As it is said – necessity is the mother of invention. When I found it physically impossible to do justice to all the responsibilities I hold, the application of the concepts of critical thinking came to be very handy. Though there is no universally accepted process flow for critical thinking, I found it convenient to develop my process flow as I progressed along the learning curve. I made mistakes – I stumbled, but every time I emerged stronger. Most importantly being a woman, I did face a lot of challenges from negotiation of deals with internal stakeholders. Apart from research, teaching and managing the two centers, I am parallel required to conduct site/field visits to understand clients' requirements and customize executive programs to best suit their needs, yet managing the P&L of the centers favorably.

Q4• Why is it important that more people work in the project management area?

We are in an era that is dynamic and highly uncertain. I consider my entire work profile as a project, that is always susceptible to the quadruple constraints of project management. The moment we consider every job as a project, we can immediately apply the principles of project management to make it happen within time, scope and budget, without sacrificing on quality. However, it is important to ensure legitimate expectations and deliverables. A Project Manager does not hone just technical knowledge and skills. Effective project managers should be able to negotiate reasonable and achievable deadlines and milestones across stakeholders, teams, and management. The fundamentals of managing a project from start to finish require a team of individuals with different talents and skills. Those people are responsible for planning and executing the project objectives and that takes more than just employees and materials. Holistic knowledge of a project lifecycle is thus a must to individuals.

Q5• How can we encourage more people to pursue project management as a career?

Education and training is the key to learning project management. I would say that they should introduce the subject right from high school. Organizations should foster existing skills of employees working in teams. More importantly attractive salaries and recognition for project managers can make the profession more acceptable.

Q6• What do you think are the top issues that project managers face today?

There is a high level of expectation at every level in the organization. One cannot be given more attention than the other – they are equally demanding. Enabling the shared leadership model is not free from challenges. There could be unintended mistakes, lack of farsightedness, strategic insights, etc., that could have detrimental impact on project or client relationships. Ambiguous plans and lack of support from top management play a crucial role when it comes to ill-

management of these challenges. Stringent deadlines, adherence to quality standards, changing customer demands, competition – all put together make the job challenging and thrilling, simultaneously. A classic disconnect happens when we fail to explain HR the depth and breadth of our activities and hence, not getting the required resource allocation. Being perpetually, resource deprived due lack of knowledge, exposure and future expectations, has been the major challenge.

Q7• Do you think there is a stereotype attached to project managers?

Yes – there are a few stereotypes that are attached to project managers. For example, often people not belonging to the domain think project managers are only executors and not decision makers or leaders. They are plan-driven and do not adapt agile methodologies and are rather inflexible. It is also often said that project managers in construction management should be male dominated, as women are unfit for hard work conditions. This sort of myths do exist.

Q8• Why is it important to celebrate international women's day?

In my opinion every day is special. Nevertheless, celebrating an international women's day appreciates the women in various field of social, economic and cultural achievements.

Q9• On international women' s day, what is the most important message you offer to project management professionals?

Critical thinking is an art, and every project manager should learn and possess it to achieve success in project management.

Vanita Bhoola

With a Doctorate in Project Risk Management and over 20 years of experience in Project Governance, Project Management, and Decision Support Systems, Dr. Vanita Bhoola works as a Professor at SPJIMR. Apart from teaching across programs at SPJIMR, she mentors students and publishes in leading international journals; she offers tailored courses across different programs at the Institute and customized management development programs (MDP). Her expertise in the area of Project Management based on prior research about company, sector and the immediate business environment that influences the business. She has published dozens of articles, research papers and case studies on project management. Her current research deals with team dynamics in project environment with emphasis on value creation, management, and governance of projects. In addition to this, she has given talks in various forums and seminars to champions of project management. She is also involved in voluntarily teaching in schools and colleges as Train the Trainer to bring awareness of the current trends of Project management in the VUCA world.

She currently heads the Center for Project Management & Principal coordinator of Executive education at SPJIMR. The Center offers PMP® Training and Certification in Advanced Project Management. Dr. Bhoola has handled training & development projects and consultancy assignments with corporate clients, such as, CGI Group Inc. (India), Pfizer India, Abott Nutrition, Kalpataru Group, Siemens India, ICICI Securities, Deutsche Bank, Procter & Gamble, Colgate-Palmolive, Tata Housing Development Company, Brigade Group, KEC International, Quality Kiosks, Mahindra & Mahindra, Verchuska Infotech and Godrej Infotech and many more. She is responsible for the short-term Executive education programs at the institute, from conversion to implantation and closure.

Courses:

- *International Project Management (being conducted for IMBA, Nyenrode)*
- *Project Management for Infrastructure / Construction / IT / Pharma / Services*
- *Project Governance*
- *Decision Modeling and Information using Spreadsheet*
- *Project Planning and Monitoring using Tools and Techniques*

Viviane De Paula
Brazil

S. PMI (São Paulo Chapter, Brazil) / Volunteer Project Manager

Q1• Describe your journey as a project management professional.

I started my career with Nokia back in 2004, when I joined the New Product Engineering team. The main deliverable of these projects were the implementation of new products in the production line. As a project manager I was responsible to integrate a multidisciplinary team; engineers, quality specialists, logistics, sourcing, production, R & D teams and marketing product managers were part of these stakeholders. After eight years I left Nokia, and joined Elekta Medical Systems, as a Latin American Project Manager, the main deliverables were the installation of cancer treatment medical devices and the implementation of a training program plan. I would integrate some multicultural, multidisciplinary and multiorganization teams and other groups of stakeholders, aimed to deliver these projects in many Latin American countries such as; Brazil, Cuba, Argentina, Venezuela, Colombia and Chile etc. I was with Elekta for four years and a half. I am also a PMI volunteer, currently I am a mentor to PMI members.

Q2• Why did you choose to become a project management professional?

I have realized that I have three great assets to become a project manager: social talent skills combined with communication and leadership abilities that could be used to deliver products and also contribute to add value to the organization.

Q3• Have you encountered any related obstacles in advancing your career?

I would not say "obstacles", but rather I' d prefer to use the word "challenges". As a project manager, I put great deal of effort to analyze and understand different groups of stakeholders considering their culture, experience, attitude, complexity, level of influence, power and also, to prepare the best strategy to communicate with them all.

The main challenge was to understand that not all stakeholders are working to the greater good of the organization, as people have their own interests. So, my main challenge was to figure out how to best navigate on a complex scenario with people having with different interests and yet, still keep focus on the organization's needs and project objectives.

Q4• Why is it important that more people work in the project management area?

Project management is not only a science but also an art that can be applied to any life situation. People get married, travel, change carriers, move to another country. These are all projects, only they don't realize it. On a professional level, project management skills can be applied to better manage teams, increase business opportunities, create new products, review business strategies, etc.

Having said that, I would argue that people do not need necessarily to work in the project management area, BUT to USE project management knowledge, skills and abilities in order to improve their work productivity.

Q5• How can we encourage more people to pursue project management as a career?

By showing them how project manager can help not only to advance their carriers but also to their lives. (read more details in the previous answer)

Q6• What do you think are the top issues that project managers face today?

Low level of organizational maturity and support in project management. Many organizations have not yet realized how project management can help to support their business goals. As a result, project managers are still struggling to implement good PM practices, for not finding the appropriate support within their own organizations.

Q7• Do you think there is a stereotype attached to project managers?

Some organizations view project managers as way too methodic, meaning lack of flexibility for always thinking/talking about processes, tools.

Q8• Why is it important to celebrate international women's day?

I dont.

Q9• On international women' s day, what is the most important message you offer to project management professionals?

That project management is a difficult career, regardless of gender. A good project manager should focus on people and communication skills in order to overcome all challenges. Gender has nothing to do with it.

Viviane de Paula

Viviane is a Brazilian Engineer with MBA in Project Management, also PMP certified with solid experience in project management in telecommunication and medical device industries for the last 15 years. Also is active PMI volunteer.

Implemented oncology hardware and software new products projects installation in Latin America by leading multidisciplinary, multi-cultural and multiorganizational teams and other groups of stakeholders.

Currently, she is working as a Program Manager of the projects. "Excellence to our customer services" aimed to improve our associates' level of satisfaction as well as implementing actions to gain more members to our PMI community.

She is a PMI mentor, as part of the PMI Mentoring Program, 2019. Knowledge sharing combined with interpersonal skills, to help others to strive in their journey.

Yvonne Butler
Australia

The Information Source / Managing Director

Q1• Describe your journey as a project management professional.

I am absolutely an "accidental project manager"! I started work in commercial law firms, established my own consulting practice, then, went into a global consulting group. We would write amazing corporate strategies and organizational transformations and give our clients fantastic advice, but were not always engaged to implement. Some organizations were successful, others were not, and I wanted to understand what was the key to successful and sustainable value creation.

After doing extensive research and talking with lots of people, I decided that project management was a critical discipline for all organisations. It became clear to me that the rigour, logic, approach to risk, time, quality and stakeholder engagement in construction, engineering and infrastructure projects all were a discipline that could and should be applied to all projects, regardless of the industry sector. I really didn't know much about how it was practiced, so I went to work for a large, independent project management company to learn more about it. You can read all about it and undertake education and training, but it isn't until you see experts at work, that one truly understands what project management is all about.

During this time I led and directed all sorts of projects and programs from IT implementations, organizational restructures, strategy and policy implementations, to change management and corporate mergers, acquisition and post-merger implementations. I worked across Defence, government departments, stock exchange listed companies and private entities. I had become a convert and advocate!

After subsequently working for two Harvard professors Robert Kaplan and David Norton, founders of the balanced scorecard, I learned the true role of governance and risk management to provide oversight to ensure the delivery of outcomes.

Q2• Why did you choose to become a project management professional?

For me, project management is the critical link between an organisation having a clear understanding of its strategic intent, how it is going to deliver on its enterprise and business objectives, and how it is going to effectively manage risks and leverage opportunities.

I believed in the profession and the contribution that project managers make so much, that I became the CEO of the Australian Institute of Project Management and a member of the Council of Delegates for the International Project Management Association.

Q3• Have you encountered any related obstacles in advancing your career?

Obstacles exist in every career, and I believe it's up to us to overcome them as individuals, teams, organisations and societies. My approach has always been to look at what's causing the obstacle (is it me or is it others?) and then consciously make the necessary changes. If I can't do it on my own, then I also look for key influencers, seek their support.

There is no doubt, however, that we need to actively practice better diversity and inclusion at all levels. This is not just a gender issue. We need diversity of thought, age, culture and personalities to change the status quo, to nurture innovation and drive change. This is rarely easy and requires each of us to be very resilient.

Q4• Why is it important that more people work in the project management area?

Our world is a world of projects, because there is no human activity without projects.

Projects change our world; they transform our visions into reality and create a future fitting both for humans and the community.

Every organisation on the planet exists to create and protect value, regardless of whether that is financial or other value. I strongly believe in the role of project management in our societies and its important role in contributing to Gross Domestic Product (GDP). Our research estimates that projects account for some 35% of GDP in developed countries, comprising mostly major capital works projects. If we can improve the delivery of these critical physical and social infrastructure projects, then we can improve our local, national and global economies.

Q5• How can we encourage more people to pursue project management as a career?

Practical advocacy; I've spoken with a lot of people all around the world and I'm yet to find many who decided during their school years, that they wanted to become a project manager.

We need to be much better at telling people what we do and the difference we make. Our professional bodies need to send consistent messages about making the link between organizational outcomes and the role that project managers play. We need to be working much more closely with governments, industry and academia to ensure that, people with real experience and appropriate project management competencies are brought into organizations as specialists and recognized for their contribution.

And of course we must work much more closely with schools and others who foster young minds. For educators, there is now a greater need for science, technology, engineering and maths (STEM) concepts to integrate with the arts (STEAM) across the wider curriculum. Teachers working in cross-curricular STEAM settings, often see their students making connections between concepts and solving problems in new and exciting ways. They demonstrate this by active engagement, their discoveries visible in enthusiastic "aha!" moments. Project managers are ultimately facilitators of outcomes within constraints, so we need to help develop balanced 'hard and soft' skills in our future workforce.

Q6• What do you think are the top issues that project managers face today?

Everyone in the world has delivered some type of project around the home or at work. So many people believe it is a generic skill that everyone has. Project management is becoming commoditized - we need to move up the value chain.

We need to drive better project leadership and project sponsorship, where people without a project management background are enabled to understand what it takes to set a project up for success and, provide valuable direction, oversight and support. Our project managers need to think and act differently; after all we are managers, not technicians.

We need project managers and sponsors to be better at:
- *Describing the vision of the destination and define what success looks like*
- *Articulating a compelling reason to get there*
- *Demonstrating a preparedness to remove barriers*
- *Questioning as an executive, not as a technician; embracing complexity*
- *Attracting, maintaining and developing project managers and project teams*
- *Recognizing and rewarding competent project managers*
- *Balancing risk and opportunity to deliver the right outcomes*
- *Thinking and acting with agility, not slavishly following a methodology*
- *Providing a safe innovation environment – capture lessons learned and openly share knowledge*
- *Demonstrate ethical and conscious governance.*

Q7• Do you think there is a stereotype attached to project managers?

Unfortunately yes.

Q8• Why is it important to celebrate international women's day?

It is beyond contention that diversity and inclusion in project teams, as in life, delivers significant benefits. If we just look at the gender aspect of diversity and inclusion, women typically:

- *Focus more on facts*
- *Process those facts more carefully and*
- *Tend to be better communicators, more innovative and therefore, very effective.*

International Women's Day seeks to help forge a gender equal world.

Celebrating women's achievements and increasing visibility, while calling out inequality on a global scale, is key.

But true gender equality is still a goal we are struggling to achieve, especially at senior executive level and on Boards of Directors. In Australia, we have an excellent example of collaboration to address this issue. Chief Executive Women (CEW) and Male Champions of Change (MCC) share a common goal to achieve gender equality and advance more women into senior leadership positions. This is a fundamental economic, business and social issue. Women and men in positions of power must work together to deliver sustainable change.

Many organisations have taken innovative approaches to shift the systems that result in inequality, but we still encounter a level of resistance to our approaches; such responses manifest as internal and public debate on issues such as: gender fatigue; the demise of meritocracy; reverse discrimination; experiences of gender-based harassment and discrimination; and the rise of identity politics. There is a view that efforts to achieve gender equality have simply 'gone too far'.

Why are we still having this conversation in 2020?

Q9•   On international women' s day, what is the most important message you offer to project management professionals?
Equality is not a women's issue, it's a business issue. Businesses must insist on diversity and inclusion in project teams. Project management professionals are essential for economies and communities to thrive.

Yvonne Butler

Having started her career with the top 4 global accounting Firms, two of the top 3 Australian law firms, top 100 ASX listed companies, global consulting firms, not for profit organisations and industry associations, Yvonne 'gets things done'.

Presently, she is Managing Director at The Information Source, where she advises boards, CEOs, and senior executives to deliver stakeholders and shareholders outcomes through Strategy to Outcomes (S2O). She is currently:

- *External Board Member Capability Acquisition and Sustainment Group (Department of Defence)*
- *Member of BoardLinks (Department of the Prime Minister in Cabinet)*
- *Lead Facilitator Mercer Board Readiness Program*
- *Board Member Royal United Services of Institute for Defence & Security Studies*
- *Graduate of Australian Institute of Company Directors*
- *Fellow of the Australian Institute of Project Management*
- *Fellow Governance Institute of Australia*
- *Fellow of the Australian Institute of Management*

Yvonne is the immediate past CEO of the Australia Institute of Project Management (AIPM) which is the peak body for project management and project managers in Australia. At AIPM, my key focus was to progression the recognition of project management as a profession in Australia through advocating the importance of portfolio, program and project management as a major contribution to GDP.

As a recognized thought leader in Strategy Execution, Project Management, Governance & Risk, Yvonne is pleased to be invited regularly to speak at international conferences and seminars, and is currently writing a book "Getting Stuff Done: The Art and Science of Strategy Execution".

About Ipek Sahra Ozguler

Ipek Sahra Ozguler graduated from the Istanbul University, Turkey with a Bachelor of Science degree in Computer Engineering and from Middle East Technical University, Turkey with an MSc degree in Software Management. As a project manager, she has more than 13 years of experience in various areas such as portfolio management, program management, project management, software management, business analysis. She became a certified PMP in 2012 and a certified SCRUM Master in 2014.

She has gained broader insights in a variety of projects across manufacturing, defence, FMCG (Cola Cola), insurance (Euler Hermes), audit (Deloitte), telecommunication, aviation and finance sectors. In addition, she has been working as an international correspondent for the PM World Journal since 2014.

Ipek is based in Istanbul, Turkey and can be contacted at ipeksahra@gmail.com. Her portfolio is published at the http://ipeksahra.strikingly.com/ and https://pmworldlibrary.net/authors/ipek-sahra-ozguler/.